PENGUIN BOOKS

THE FIRST DECADE

Vivy Yusof started blogging about random things and, a decade later, has a fashion empire. She co-founded the FashionValet Group in 2010 with her boyfriend and has grown the multi-million dollar company into a household name in her country, Malaysia.

Her brand dUCk is the largest modest fashion brand in Asia and was the first to collaborate with international brands like Disney, Mattel, Sephora and many others. Things went so well that she decided to marry that boyfriend. They now have four kids together and are still in disbelief.

A law graduate from the London School of Economics, Vivy would have much preferred if she had learnt software engineering instead. She has been an A-student all her life, and even took her SPM and A-Levels simultaneously, something she would never recommend to others.

Vivy Yusof has 1.8 million followers on Instagram and 247,000 subscribers on her YouTube channel. She has been featured in many local and international publications, including *Business of Fashion*, *The New York Times* and *Forbes*. She was also named as one of Forbes 30 Under 30, and selected as a Young Global Leader by World Economic Forum. Her parents still tell people about that.

The First Decade
My Journey from Blogger to Entrepreneur

Vivy Yusof

PENGUIN BOOKS

An imprint of Penguin Random House

PENGUIN BOOKS

USA | Canada | UK | Ireland | Australia
New Zealand | India | South Africa | China | Southeast Asia

Penguin Books is part of the Penguin Random House group of companies
whose addresses can be found at global.penguinrandomhouse.com

Published by Penguin Random House SEA Pte Ltd
9, Changi South Street 3, Level 08-01,
Singapore 486361

First published in Penguin Books by Penguin Random House SEA 2022

Copyright © Vivy Yusof 2022

All rights reserved

10 9 8 7 6 5 4 3 2 1

The views and opinions expressed in this book are the author's own and the
facts are as reported by her which have been verified to the extent possible,
and the publishers are not in any way liable for the same.

ISBN 9789815127959

Typeset in Garamond by MAP Systems, Bangalore, India

www.penguin.sg

To every hopeful entrepreneur.

And I guess my kids, since every mom author mentions their kids . . .

Contents

Chapter 1

How It All Began

'Vivy, what are you doing?'

There I was, seven years old, in a classroom, when the teacher called me out. The other thirty-five pairs of eyes turned to me.

'Uh, nothing,' I answered nervously, shoving things inside my desk drawer.

My heart was beating fast, worried that I'd get caught. Let's face it, I wasn't paying attention in class. I had *work* to do, Teacher. As she stared at me, I quickly covered my things with some books inside the drawer. Eyes straight at her, body not moving except my hands, which were hidden underneath the desk.

What was I hiding?

A friendship bracelet I was making to sell. It was multi-coloured and I had promised the customer (my classmate) that I would get it done by today. This was more important to me than what 9×12 equalled to.

'If I catch you doing something else again, you can stand outside the classroom,' the teacher warned me with stern eyes.

I nodded and kept quiet.

Inside, I was thinking, Well, if I sit outside, then I can actually finish the bracelet.

And there you go, the entrepreneur in me came out at the early age of seven.

The Start of My Decade

October 2010. I was twenty-two.

It was a rainy afternoon. The clouds were heavy, and the skies were grey. Traffic was moving very slowly. The only things moving fast were the wipers wiping off the rain. Drivers were honking, faces clearly impatient. Bet they were all wishing they were home watching TV instead. One of them was the driver in my car, my now-husband-then-boyfriend, Fadza.

I looked at him.

Ahh, the love of my life.

We had met in 2005 in London, where we both studied. Introduced by a mutual friend, it was *not* love at first sight. I found him obnoxious because he barely uttered a word to me, and he found me bimbotic because I was carrying a designer bag. Well, God works in mysterious ways, because a year later, we met randomly at Bristol University; I was on a field trip there with my college and he was going there for an enrolment interview. What are the odds? Two Malaysians on the same street in a foreign city at the same split second.

'Vivy!' I heard a voice calling me, so I turned.

At that moment, we were facing each other across the street, separated by the cars on the road. It was winter: he was cleaned-up, wearing a suit and a scarf around his neck, and I was in my coat with the wind blowing through my hair. It was like a K-drama scene.

'Oh, hey. Fadza, right?' I asked, acting aloof but really thinking *oooh, he looks good.*

Be cool, be cool.

From that moment, we added each other on Friendster (I KNOW, RIGHT!) and we started getting to know each other online. We would go on MSN Messenger (again, I KNOW RIGHT!) and get excited when we saw the other online. After a while, he asked me out to a movie.

While at the counter to buy our tickets, he took out his wallet and said, 'One ticket to *You, Me and Dupree*, please.'

One ticket?

He then looked at me after paying, motioning me to get my own ticket.

WHAT.

On our first date, he makes me pay for my own ticket?

What kind of lousy date was this?

But funnily enough, I found him so interesting because he wasn't like the other guys who were sweet-talkers. He was different—so confident, so nonchalant. Over time, we let our guards down and grew really fond of one another. He became a huge part of my life since the start of university, and we've never looked back ever since. It was only after we started liking each other that he started treating me like a princess. Walking me to my university, seeing me off right to my door, making sure I ate every meal, accompanying me to everything—he was always there for me. And yes, every movie ticket was paid for.

Our entire university lives revolved around one another. I read law at the London School of Economics (LSE), and he studied aeronautical engineering at Imperial College in London. We both planned to experience working there after graduation but there was an economic downturn then, so it was really difficult to get a job. I remember I really wanted a writer's job at *Vogue*, so I naively went to their office and asked how I could get one. I didn't get it, obviously. Fadza got offers from companies back home, and in the end, chose to work at Deloitte Malaysia, while I dabbled in the construction industry under my dad's wings.

The two of us packed up our lives in London and returned to Malaysia, introduced our families to one another and voila, the rest is history.

I smiled thinking of all this, reminiscing how far we've come and still going strong in our relationship.

My sweet thoughts of us were interrupted when he sighed in the car.

'Seriously, you really need to go to this shop?' he asked for the tenth time.

For the tenth time, I squirmed. 'Sorry, I *really* need to check it out.'

No, it wasn't an emergency.

It was a top. *hides face* A specific top that I wanted. No, *needed*.

We had gone to a few shops already but none of them had spoken to me. You should really see Fadza's face when I say these things to him. 'You mean these clothes . . . speak to you?'

Umm . . . yes. Yours don't?

Trust me, I wanted the traffic to move just as much as he did. Being stuck in a car with an angry driver isn't exactly a five-star rated adventure. Finally the traffic light turned green. Phew, thank you, God. One car turned, second car turned . . . we were next. Boom, the traffic light turned red again.

What.

The.

This traffic light was sabotaging my relationship.

At this point, Fadza was turning red. *Look away, look away*, I told myself, head turned to the window. 'Ooh, look, a tree,' I said meekly. He did not look at that tree. Tree be like, 'Don't bring me into this'.

'This is going to take forever. Why can't all these shops be in one place?' he asked in frustration, out loud.

Oh.

Hmmm . . . why *couldn't* these shops be in one place? Instead of going to each shop one by one, what *if* they were all together? That will save everyone time and effort.

Oooh!

What Fadza had asked triggered a spark in my brain.

'Even better, have all these shops in one place *online*. Then we don't have to be stuck in a bad traffic jam like this one!' he sighed again.

Ooooooohhhh!

This is the part where you have to imagine a lightbulb flickering excitedly on top of my head.

We both kept quiet. I think he, too, was thinking about this more seriously. It was almost like our brains were sending signals to each other and going *Ting!* Our eyes locked, and if this was a romantic Whatsapp message, this is where the heart emoticons would come out. Except, this wasn't romantic. It was even better.

We may have just found a business idea.

I'd been waiting for this moment. I'd been wanting to be an entrepreneur since I was in Mom's womb, probably in there wondering if it's forty weeks yet. Come on, get me out of here, I need to register my company.

Little Vivy

The school scene is just one of the instances I remember when Little Vivy showed her entrepreneurial interest. Mom said that when I was a toddler, I loved playing with my Lego blocks, building towers from my imagination. Clearly, I had big ambitions for myself. She said I loved any toy that had to do with running a business. I'd pretend I was a shop owner, lay down all the toys as my inventory, and make Mom buy things over and over again while I clicked the buttons on the cashier. I would line up my teddy bears one by one and make them 'take care' of each aisle in my 'shop'. Even on my report card, my kindergarten teacher wrote, 'Vivy needs to learn more patience and be less bossy with her friends'. Hey, you see bossy, I see a future leader. #selflove

My childhood made my parents realize that I was going to be an entrepreneur. Either that, or a really bossy person.

Both happened. Hee.

In school, I would convince all my friends to order a friendship bracelet from me. During lunch, I'd go around asking if they wanted one, and I would change my own bracelets every day—influencer marketing since 1994, ahem. I'd take down their colour choices, buy thread after school and spend my days tying each thread, one by one. I remember having a logbook of orders. I was determined this was going to be a big business, so I bought the biggest notebook because obviously everyone needed a friendship bracelet. I grew frustrated that I wasn't filling the book fast enough, so I started writing in bigger fonts and taking up more lines per order to make it seem like I had so many pages of orders. Pretty soon, I had forced all my friends to buy a bracelet, and I was getting responses like, 'No, Vivy, I do not need a fifth bracelet.' Okay, but are you sure?

Business closed pretty soon, because, well, it was labour-intensive and I was running out of friends, relatives and friends' relatives to sell bracelets to. Also, I had to start learning division.

That didn't stop me, though. When I was nine, I started writing a book. I was so influenced by Sweet Valley Kids (DO YOU GUYS REMEMBER?!) that I started writing stories of my own. I turned that into a business, too. I would write the story in my school exercise book and pass it around for my classmates to read, charging them fifty cents each time. I even levelled up. I discovered a friend who could draw really well and made her draw in the book. Now there were pictures in the book, so I started charging people one dollar to read it. I even cut out 'library cards' for people to subscribe to my little library of one book. Subscription model, ahem.

That's when my parents discovered my love for writing.

In university, I started another business: making scrapbooks! I vaguely remember getting a law degree from LSE, but oh, the memories of cutting paper into shapes and pasting them on a cardboard still thrills me. I loved making something out of nothing, an empty paper becoming a memory immortalized, of someone's birthday or someone's anniversary—that seemed like magic to me.

As a child, my dad would never let us buy greeting cards because he wanted us to make these cards from scratch: handmade cards come from the heart, he said. We would have to buy the manila cards, the coloured papers, write the messages ourselves and design everything. My dad still has a folder of the cards my sister and I would make for him for his birthday. Over the years, the cards got more and more creative—pop-up art, poems, photos, little envelopes within the card that he had to open. I remember that I loved making all these cool cards and thinking about how to make them better and better each year—innovation! I think this honed my creativity since younger days, and the love for product development and creating something.

I started a Facebook page called Vee Scrap Pages and waited for it to get traction. Some orders trickled in, mostly from the boys at university who were too lazy to make romantic cards for their girlfriends. That worked well for me! In between my law classes, I'd make these scrapbooks and Fadza would help me too. But that business folded because Fadza didn't want to help me cut flowers any more, and I soon realized it's cheaper to buy a card than to make one—the costs of my paper, stationery, glitter, sequins and printing photos didn't even begin to be justified . . . Yeah, if there's anything you take away from my book here, it's this: don't start a scrapbooking business.

Growing up, I kept experimenting with businesses. From school till uni, I started and folded many of these. But what really stayed constant and stuck with me throughout was my love for writing. I would write newspaper articles here and there as a child, and then one fine day in uni, my friend Sofia suggested I start a blog.

'You mean like write about myself?' I asked her, with a disapproving look.

At that time, there was no social media. Blogging was *the* social media. I loved reading other blogs but felt that I wasn't conceited enough to have one of my own and to write about myself. Apparently, I was. #thanksforbuyingmybook

Sofia set it up anyway and encouraged me to start blogging.

'Hmmm okay, let's see what this is all about', I got curious. My hands kept typing as if it was the easiest thing to do, and I soon realized that I really enjoyed writing. I kept on going but from time to time I'd think, 'Gosh, this is so lame.'

What I thought was 'so lame' turned out to be the reason for all that I have right now. Blogging allowed me to express myself and connected me to wonderful fellow bloggers and readers, opening up a whole world of opportunities for me. Careful what you call 'so lame'.

I kept on blogging. I wrote every day while I was at university in London. About the randomest things—fashion, food, travel, anything funny that happened that day, falling in love with a boy. That boy was Fadza, of course, but in my blog, I named him Dean.

I was so paranoid that my dad would find out about this blog, which would mean finding out about the parties I went to in the university. I made the blog anonymous in the beginning. I pixelated the faces and didn't reveal anyone's name, not even mine. I knew my dad would be so angry if he found out I was going out here and there. *This blog must not be discovered by my dad. Protect it at all costs!*

Everything went well. He had no idea about it. So I kept on writing and writing for years.

For my graduation, my parents flew to London to celebrate this moment. My dad sat me down to give me 'the talk'. You know, the talk about life and becoming an adult now that I'd graduated, and all the possible career options there are to discuss.

Suddenly, he paused. 'Also, you should continue writing. You have a gift.'

I'm sorry, what?

No. No way. He cannot know about the blog. Maybe he's talking about something else.

'What do you mean?' I managed to croak.

'Your blog. I know about it.'

I gulped. Flashbacks of my posts about going clubbing (very rarely, okay!) and parties wearing tube dresses came flooding to my brain. I cannot imagine what my dad felt reading through all those posts.

This was it.

This was how I was going to die.

'You're . . . not mad?' I asked quietly.

'I was young once, too. But remember, your dad knows everything.'

Such thriller-worthy words from a father to a daughter, but that was when I realized my dad was the coolest dad in the world. He knew my cheeky side and didn't like it, but he was patient. He let me live my university days, but he kept a close eye. He could have easily been mad at me and that would have stopped me from blogging entirely, because I would be too scared. And if I had stopped blogging, my life would have been so different. I would not have amassed a following. I would not have gathered a community that is so supportive of me and my dreams. I would not have been the Vivy you know today.

I love my dad for not breaking that path for me, and just allowing me to flourish where I enjoyed the most. Writing was the beginning of my proper career and I hadn't yet known that at that point. When I had my dad's blessing for the blog, I let everything loose. I started revealing myself and my face, and I wrote more freely and more authentically, because I had my parents rooting for me. Not only that, they even told me I had a gift for writing. So I carried on, honing that 'gift'. I grew to become one of the most popular bloggers in my country, and I had thousands of views every day, which gave me the motivation to keep writing.

The party posts stopped, though.

I mean, my dad was cool but not THAT cool.

A Local Brands Platform

Okay, come back inside the car. Back to our lightbulb moment.

Something within us just clicked and we looked at each other.

'Are you thinking what I'm thinking?' Fadza asked me.

To start this amazing platform business and to make it a billion-dollar company and get married and live on our own island?

'Yes!' I said.

And off we went to a coffee shop to discuss this. We wasted absolutely no time. Forget that top I wanted.

I still remember us sitting there, asking the waiter if we could borrow a pen. Immediately, we drew a vision for this 'billion-dollar' business. On a piece of tissue paper from Coffee Bean. We googled 'how to start an online website' on our phones and called the first company on the page. The company we found was called Netbuilder, and it could provide services for creating the website, checkout page, the backend and the payment gateway, too. What's a payment gateway? Don't know, but sounds important. Set up a meeting ASAP. Done!

Okay, so now what were we going to sell? We decided in the car earlier to be a house of many brands, a one-stop centre where people could shop a few brands at once. Genius! We needed an edge though, something unique, so we decided to only sell local brands since there wasn't anything like this at the time. I was a customer at some of them, so I thanked myself for being a shopaholic and started making calls to them. Done!

How were we going to market this website? My blog! I already had a following there and the readers seem to gravitate to my posts on fashion. Maybe they'll buy what I sell, too. Okay, so we're going to sell clothes through my blog. Got it. Done!

Now, what will we call this website? Young and in love, naturally we wanted something cheesy with our initials in it. Fadza and Vivy, F and V. We agreed pretty fast that F should be Fashion because we wanted people to immediately know what the website sold. The V was tricky. We went through the dictionary. Vaccine, Vacuum, Vampire, Vagina, Vapour. All really, umm . . . good choices.

In the end, it was between Village and Valet. FashionVillage or FashionValet? We decided 'Valet' would be more suitable because a valet represented a service. We were delivering items to customers to make their lives easier; they didn't have to leave their house, they just had to click buttons and we would send parcels right to their doorstep. A luxury service, like a car valet. Okay, FashionValet it is!

The problem was that the domain was not available to register. We searched for the domain www.fashionvalet.com—it was a drycleaning website in the US.

'FashionValet.net is available,' Fadza said.

'Oh yes! That sounds even cooler. Let's take it,' I said, feeling like I had made the coolest decision ever.

Okay, website name, done. Website domain, done.

'Okay, what else?' we asked each other.

Oh right, money.

We needed money.

Where can we buy that?

RM 100,000 to Start

Okay. We were a couple of twenty-two-year-olds. Yes, Fadza and I come from comfortable families and our parents are well-off. *They* were well-off, but we weren't.

We had little to no savings. Financial literacy was never taught in school so I never really thought about savings or investments, growing up. I lived with my parents, so I took that for granted. The reality was that no bank was going to fund us, nobody was just going to hand two kids a large sum of money, and we had no assets to offer in return, either. After searching under every couch in the house for some loose change, we realized we needed some help with this. Bear in mind, this was in 2010—there was not much funding going around for startups, unlike the scene now, where people encourage entrepreneurship and are offering money to whoever has a good idea. Venture capitalists and angel investors were unknown terms at that point.

We didn't want to do this, but we did what every entrepreneur in that era did—borrow money.

In our case, we went to the people we trusted the most—our family members.

I went to my dad to ask to borrow my portion of the capital.

'Let me understand this. You are asking me if you can start an online shop . . . with your boyfriend?' a pair of very serious eyes looked at me.

I gulped.

'Well, he's more a *friend* . . .' Lie. 'We're not that close . . .' Lie again. 'And I've been thinking about this business for a while now.' Lie some more.

Wow, great start to this blessed business, Vivy, I thought. *Shut up, brain.*

I didn't want to ask him and burden him, but who else could I turn to but my dad? But as much as he loves me, he wouldn't just hand me or my sister money every time we asked. No way. We had to always present our case, with a presentation of what we needed it for and how we were going to pay it back. He taught us that money doesn't come easy and that (1) you should never borrow money from people and (2) if you really must do it, you must be honourable and have a plan about how to pay it back. *Never owe anyone anything*, he would always remind us.

Fadza and I had to present the idea of FashionValet to him, why we were perfect as business partners and why this business was a viable one that could be huge. He liked the business in the end and believed in the ecommerce boom, coupled with my online following, but as any father, was not so thrilled about my boyfriend and I being partners.

He grilled us some more, asked some hard questions, called for multiple family meetings, prayed, consulted his finance manager, asked the finance manager to interview Fadza and I, consulted another manager, asked that manager to interview us. I mean, it's arguable that I could have got it more easily from a bank . . .

He said yes in the end, but as a chaperone, he would come in as a shareholder with a small stake so it wouldn't be just a boyfriend–girlfriend company. So it was Fadza and I as majority shareholders, individually, and my dad as a minority shareholder. I'm sure Fadza had dreamt of this beautiful day, being in business with his girlfriend . . . and her father. I guess this was my dad's way of telling Fadza, 'You better marry her.' So yeah, our beautiful love story, guys.

Okay, so with that done, my dad agreed to loan me RM 50,000. Fadza also forked out RM 50,000 from his savings and borrowings from his generous brother, who helped him.

Together, we now had RM 100,000.

Please, everybody, make way for the richest twenty-two-year-olds in the world.

Setting Up

'What do you mean this air-conditioner costs RM 2,000?' I asked the contractor.

We were standing in the brand-new office that we had rented. It was above my dad's office, because well, that was another condition so he could keep an eye on us young lovers with raging hormones.

The office was bare. We had to pay for the wiring, the plugs, everything! 'This is ridiculous,' I thought, 'I'm already paying rent—shouldn't all these things come with it?' The floor was uneven but levelling it would have cost too much, so I decided we should just carpet the whole thing. I chose the cheapest carpet material.

'Got anything cheaper?' I asked the contractor.

'You can get this red one. No one wants red colour carpet,' he said to me, pointing to a hideous red on the swatch card.

Red carpet it was!

I just ignored that judgy face my contractor made.

Renovating for the first time made me realize how expensive everything was. I needed to buy air conditioners, and we needed a few units for the different rooms in that unit. That's maybe RM 10,000 gone. Just for . . . air! From that day on, I have never taken air conditioners for granted ever again. I greet mine every morning. 'Hello, air-con. You're expensive.'

The rest I kept as bare as possible. Furniture—we bought the cheapest plastic stuff from IKEA and assembled it ourselves. Look at that lady at the counter trying to con us with her, 'Did you want to add assembling cost?'. We also went to Jalan Kenanga to buy all the office equipment like racks (we bought the cheapest ones and that was a mistake because they had big gaps between them so the stock would just fall everywhere in between racks), mannequins, plastic, sticker labels, railings, hangers, and all of that.

Then we needed to invest in studio equipment—a camera, some lighting, a backdrop—so we went to a building in Kuala Lumpur known for selling these. 'Don't dress so nice,' Fadza warned me. I wore the most basic t-shirt and slippers, and still got a, 'Why are you so dressed up?' from him. Okay, so lose the six bracelets and pearl necklace then?

We haggled our way into buying a good enough Nikon model camera and some basic lenses. Lighting, we had no idea. We weren't photographers; I thought the sun gave lighting. We bought one light that looked like a huge umbrella. Not sure if it was the right one, but hey, it made a click sound whenever we took a photo, so it must be working well. Worried about our bank balance (I mean, we had not even bought the *actual* stock we wanted to sell yet!), we decided not to buy a professional backdrop. We decided, 'Let's just use white bedsheet and tape it from the wall to floor.' Voila, our studio was ready! Sure, the photos were yellow with uneven lighting. They had like a gradient because the one light we bought could only shine light from one side. Maybe some people would think it's artsy? Our bank balance confirmed it was artsy.

The office was coming together—red carpet and expensive air-conditioner and all. We had everything we needed. Mom even donated a fridge, bless her kind heart.

Now, all we needed were the actual items to sell.

Time to speak to some designers to convince them to join our platform as vendors.

We had a bit of money left, and we were apportioning which designers to buy stock from, when my dad's finance manager, Ivy, overheard our conversation (my dad plants them everywhere, so they just 'show up' randomly. Like, 'Oops I left a file.' In someone else's office on another floor?).

'Why are you buying their stock?' Ivy asked me.

'Er, because I need to sell the stock,' I answered.

'Yes, I know, but why are you *buying* them?' she asked again.

Is this lady okay? I thought my dad said she was smart.

'Because I have to *take* them from the designers and *sell* them on our website . . .' I explained slowly, as if talking to a child.

'That is a lot of inventory risk from others to you. You should just consign the products,' she said.

'Consign?' I ask, intrigued.

'Consignment. When you take their products first, and only pay them after you've made a sale. If you don't make a sale, you return the goods to them,' she schooled me. 'You know the consignment model, right?'

I laughed. 'Of course I do!'

Wow, there's such a thing?

That sounds good. Let's go with whatever she just said. *googles con-sign-ment*

With that, I was ready to meet the designers. I had managed to convince my best friend, Asma', to join me as a fashion buyer. If there is one person who has helped Fadza and I the most in our startup, it's this girl. I owe her so much, for everything that she has sacrificed for me. She left her magazine journalist job and took a leap of faith at FashionValet. She had a family business of making beautiful wedding cakes with her mom, so during the day, she would work with us, and at night, she would go home and stay up till the wee hours to create these amazing five-tier wedding cakes. How she got her energy is beyond me, and till today, I am always in awe of her. My dad, especially, loved

Asma' because having her meant that Fadza and I were never alone in the office together. #halaloffice

Fadza still had his day job so he would come early in the morning to help us prep and late evening to continue whatever we were working on. So most of the time, the day-to-day running of the business was up to Asma' and me—two girls in their heels, ready to conquer the world. Asma' agreed to a RM 1,000 salary (we joke now that she should really hire a manager to do her negotiations in the future), and Fadza and I drew a monthly salary of RM 500 in the second year. As you can imagine, we certainly had no plans to move out from our parents' homes. #freeshelterandfood

Signing On Vendors

Signing on vendors wasn't as fast and simple as we had thought it would be. Asma' and I were going door to door, knocking on shops to introduce them to FashionValet and begging them to give us their manager's phone numbers because we knew that our emails would always be ignored. Many were sceptical in the beginning, so it wasn't easy.

'You want to take my clothes and sell them? But I don't even know you.'

'Who exactly would buy clothes from a computer screen?'

'Who else have you signed on?'

'But you don't even have a website yet . . .'

'Consignment? What does that mean?'

Phew. I wasn't the only one who didn't know what consignment was.

These were all hard questions, and we grew thick skins to answer all of them. We started going with business cards that we had printed to look professional, but the truth was we didn't have a website, we didn't have anything! Just one mannequin and a cold office.

I, very unprofessionally, did up a mockup of the website on a piece of paper, and this was the only thing we had to convince the designers. The number of times we went to the back office to meet with managers of boutiques, full of hope that they would believe in FashionValet and take a chance on us! Some managers would make us wait very long, so Asma' and I would sit at the front of the store surrounded by these beautiful clothes. *Let me sell you on my website,* I would think as I ran my fingers through them. We were young and hopeful, and I remember that feeling very well—the feeling of excitement mixed with hope so bad that it was nauseating. That feeling of believing in something so much that your heart would just be crushed when someone didn't feel the same way about it. We managed to convince a few of them, but there were more rejections.

It was taking too long to convince boutiques/designers, so I thought of a different route. Instead of getting the smaller ones, let's try for the big ones first. Very nervously, I took my phone and searched for Datuk Radzuan Radziwill on my phone. He is this amazing designer who, till today, dresses VIPs and the royal families. Lucky for me, he made my sister's wedding dress, so I had met him a few times during her fittings.

'Hello?' my voice was shaking as he picked up the phone on the other line.

I cannot mess this up, I cannot mess this up.

He was warm and friendly, and my heart rate slowly went back to normal. I explained to him the concept of FashionValet and to my surprise, he answered, 'Sounds interesting. Come to my boutique and tell me more.'

I went over the next day and the meeting was a success. I had signed on one of the biggest designers in the country. I couldn't believe my luck. I remember jumping up and down with Asma' and immediately calling Fadza on the phone to tell him the good news.

After getting him on board, it was easier to sign on the rest. I gained more confidence when meeting new brands as I had done it so many times already. I would walk door to door in malls and on the streets of Bangsar, repeating the script I had prepared about FashionValet. It came so naturally after a while, I was probably chanting it in my sleep!

Asma' and I were meeting several brands a day, and we realized it took more than two meetings per brand to close the deal, so you can imagine the amount of meetings we had. We were doing this frantically, prior to the launch of the website, and if I recall correctly, we had signed thirty brands in the first month. However, only ten were ready with stock, so FashionValet officially debuted with ten local brands.

Oh, I still remember receiving the first batch of clothes. It was a pink and black collection from this one brand called PU3. The pieces were absolutely beautiful, and I remember hugging them tight when they arrived. Our first-ever stock. This is really happening! PU3/T1/ BLACK/001—we labelled them one by one manually, wrote each product code with love. I still remember the first product code. This was the most horrible way of stock-keeping, by the way, never do it this way! But back then, that was the only way I knew to do it, and I was convinced that I was a warehousing genius.

The three of us took one of each piece as a sample for the photoshoot. We steamed each item, took photos of it in our makeshift studio and uploaded them to my laptop. We did not want to spend extra money on models so one poor mannequin worked overtime as we took off its arms and legs more than a thousand times. After a hard day's work of shooting photos, I would spend the nights uploading the items on the website backend. I had to teach myself Photoshop and edit each photo, resize it, edit the brightness and contrast, you know really *professional* stuff.

Now there are apps to do all these in two seconds.

I'm slightly bitter about that.

After that, I would add each item's description, measurements (taken literally on the floor with measuring tape), price, photos and upload them on the website. During this time, Fadza and I barely slept, both of us in our own homes typing and editing away till morning to make sure the website was ready for the launch with products.

We Had to Be the First

One day, I was meeting a brand to onboard them, and the designer said, 'Oh, someone came last week to pitch the same idea.'

Sorry, what did you just say?

If there's anything you have to know about me is that I'm very competitive. Even in school, I had to make sure I was the first to finish an exam, or the first to put up my hand whenever the teacher asked anything. I really wonder how I had any friends.

I was so competitive that I overlapped my final year of high school and first year of A-Levels. I took my SPM exams (end of high school exams) and A-Level exams at the same time, flying back and forth between Kuala Lumpur—where I did my high school—and the UK, where I did my A-Levels. That's right, I was studying for two different years in the same year and had enrolled myself in two different schools located in two different countries at the same time. The reason for this is because (a) I'm crazy and (b) I didn't want to wait to start my A-Levels. High school in Malaysia finishes in December but A-Levels in the UK start in September. So instead of waiting nine months for the next intake, I decided to start earlier instead. I had to convince both schools—I applied for A-Levels in the UK with my mid-year exam results, and I had to write in black and white that if I failed any exam, I would have to start over.

Both schools accepted my request, and so the pressure was on me to prove myself. In the UK, I went to my A-Level classes during the day, and in the evenings, I would study for my SPM exams using the textbooks that I had packed with me from Malaysia. I studied for all ten subjects for SPM, plus four subjects for my A-Levels. I flew to Malaysia to take my SPM exam in December, and then flew back to the UK to take my A-Levels in January. My parents were worried, my teachers were worried, my friends thought I was crazy. No one put this on me except for myself—I was in such a high to challenge myself.

In the end, I beat all odds and got all As. For both my SPM and A-Levels! My parents were beaming proud, and we all let out big sighs of relief. Them more than me, because they didn't have to pay for an additional year of school fees! #phew

I wanted to grow up fast so I worked my butt off. That's how competitive I was, and I needed no motivation from anyone. I was in competition with no one, just myself, and even at *that*, I had to win.

So when I heard there might be other people beating me to launch something similar, my competitive spirit was triggered. I needed to make sure I was the first to launch this multi-brand website in Malaysia.

After the meeting, I called Fadza immediately, 'We need to launch ASAP.'

'No, we need to make sure everything is in order,' Fadza replied.

Anybody working at FashionValet would know Fadza and I are very different. I'm the determined and impatient one, who wants things yesterday, and Fadza is the sensible and calm one, who tones me down. We're perfect together.

'Okay, there's no such thing. Do you want us to be second? Do you want another website beating us to this?' I asked him.

I'm pretty sure he said something sensible and calm, but I wasn't listening because I was already emailing our web developer Netbuilder to see if we can bump up the timeline.

'Dear Miss Vivy, as mentioned earlier, this project will take six months. Please don't hesitate to contact us for any other queries. Sincerely, Afandi,' the email said.

I do have other queries, Afandi.

I called their office and spoke to Afandi. 'We need to launch by November. How can we make it happen?'

'November is next month. There are a lot of processes involved in building this website. We cannot rush the project.'

'Okay, what can we do to make it happen, though? I could learn how to code. I'm a fast learner. I could work from your office every day.'

'Please do not do that, Miss Vivy. We do not want that.' He answered so fast that it almost hurt my feelings.

They said it will take six months, but I knew the game—everyone keeps a margin to be safe, but things can be done so fast if people want them to.

I pressed on.

I looked at their scope for the six-month timeline and studied it. I told them I could forego some things and just go with a super basic website. I let go of certain features that I thought we could develop later on. There was also a time period for training us on how to use the website and the system. I told them I didn't need a month for that, teach us in one day. They were shocked but they said okay.

After negotiating the scope back and forth, drumroll please . . . the website did launch in one month.

Ta-daaaa!

I felt like a winner in this competition with Afandi, the unwilling participant.

'See, we can, what,' I said to the Netbuilder team, laughing.

They did not laugh back.

I'm pretty sure they tried very hard not to scream at me whenever I'd call to check in on the progress, but they were a very sweet team that tried their best to accommodate us as clients. I miss you, Afandi. You were on my speed dial, much to your dismay, and I'd like to thank you for never hanging up on me. And I hope that you could see that when pressured, you did what you thought you couldn't do, so you're welcome, okay bye.

The night before the launch, we gathered for last-minute preparation in the office—Fadza, myself and, of course, Asma'. My sister, Intan, was there to lend support and entertain us. My best friend, Ajjrina, was there too, despite her own mountain-load of work. Our friend Ron was there, helping us change clothes on the naked mannequin, but he really didn't look like he minded it at all.

Everyone was helping us that night and I was overwhelmed with feelings. Love, excitement, exhaustion, nerves—everything rolled into one. But the biggest was the feeling of hope. Hope that people would like it, hope that people would buy something, hope that I was doing the right thing. There is no guarantee in life. No manual to tell you this is right and this is wrong. No script that tells you what to do. My dad always told me to write my own script, so I did just that. I did not know if this script of mine would become something worth watching, but the only way to find out was to go on.

This was it. This was the beginning of a new chapter for Fadza and me. This was the eve of our business actually starting. This was the day we were about to become entrepreneurs. This was the day we had all been working so hard towards, and there was no looking back from here. All those friendship bracelets I weaved, the books I made my friends rent, all those scrapbooks I made for others—they were little signs that led me to this day. Little signs that nudged me to believe that I was born to be an entrepreneur.

The next day, I was alone in the office, facing my laptop and staring at the email I was supposed to reply to, to make the website go live. Fadza had to go to work, and Asma' had to help her mother with a cake.

'You ready?' a message from Fadza beeped. He had been refreshing the website URL, as excited as I had been to see FashionValet's debut into the world.

'Ready!' I replied.

I hit 'Send Email' to give Netbuilder the instruction to launch the site.

And with that, on 16 November 2010, literally only *one* month after Fadza and I had had the idea in the car, FashionValet.net was launched to the public, thus launching Fadza and I as entrepreneurs.

This was Day 1.

Little did we know that our lives were about to change forever.

Chapter 2

The Early Days

'He's looking, he's looking!' I whispered to Asma' as we giggled, running out of the Apple store.

We didn't have much money left, so marketing in the early days meant going to Apple stores and putting up the FashionValet.net website on every Mac in their store. They got loads of traffic at their stores and this way, their customers would *have* to see the FashionValet website before they could do other things with the computers in the store. We would get dagger eyes from the store managers (hence me asking Asma' to hurry up and leave), but it wasn't illegal, so . . .

We also printed out FashionValet.net flyers on postcard-sized paper, and went from home to home to put one through every mailbox. If you saw us, you would've laughed. Fadza driving and us girls going out to the mailboxes and back in the car, then driving an inch further and out and in again, and repeat. After we got tired, we resorted to the malls. We went from store to store and restaurant to restaurant to ask if we could put a stack of FashionValet.net flyers on their cashier counter. I was surprised that a lot of them said yes!

The early days were the best and somehow the busiest. It was just the three of us, splitting roles among each other. Fadza was still working at Deloitte, so during the day, it was mostly Asma' and I. But pretty soon, going out to sign on brands and designers took up a lot of our time so we'd come back rushing to pack orders and worrying that we'd miss the courier cut-off time for the day. We needed to hire one more person, so a girl named Anis came into our lives. It was hilarious because we didn't know what her title would be. I mean she'd be doing a bit of marketing, a bit of product uploads and a bit of packing orders so we couldn't limit her to one department. This was, after all, a startup, so you would have to be a jack of all trades for a while. So Anis became Brand Executive, whatever that meant. The interview took five minutes, not because it went really well, but because I had no idea what to ask!

'How are you?' I asked nervously. I mean, my first-ever staff interview! It's so much easier to be the person answering because you don't have to lead the conversation and think of smart questions.

'Good, Ms Vivy,' she answered, nervous too.

We were both nervous. *Can we please end this misery now?*

But wow, she called me 'Ms Vivy'. I felt like a real grownup boss here. I could get used to this.

'Umm, so you can pack orders?'

'I can learn.'

'Can you steam clothes?'

'I can learn.'

'Can you write invoices?'

'I can learn.'

'Okay, you're hired.'

Sounds like a stellar candidate to me.

Anis came to work the very next day. I found out that she had just had a baby so she brought her baby along to the office. There was no HR policy whatsoever at the time. How was I to know the dos and don'ts of this? So Asma', I, Anis and her baby hung out together, packing orders and sorting out the stock.

We did a bit of everything, without a clue if we were doing it right or not. But it seemed to be working, because our sales were increasing and customers were growing. Our sales were almost at RM 1 million in the first year! With just Facebook, email newsletters and my blog (oh, and Apple stores, thank you Apple), this all seemed too good to be true.

Fadza Joins Full-time

After a few months of running FashionValet, Fadza felt more and more left out because he wasn't around as much as I was. There was this burning desire in him to leave his job at Deloitte. I could imagine this decision to be a heavy one, one that a lot of people would face in their lifetime. Do you leave a stable income job for something that isn't sure? But is anything ever sure?

To Fadza, the decision was clear. His heart was permanently here since the day FashionValet had started. He knew that he wanted to grow this business, not only in early mornings and late evenings, but every moment of the day. He could no longer concentrate at work because he was thinking about FashionValet most of the time. And me, I hope.

He knew he had to go. His heart had already left Deloitte.

But his dad was not thrilled about his decision.

'What do you mean you want to leave your job?' he asked Fadza.

'The business is going well, and I want to focus on it,' Fadza answered.

'I send you far away to study in London, and you come back and sell women's clothes with your girlfriend?' he would say to Fadza.

I mean, the man was not wrong. But #ouch.

We laugh about this now but back then, it was not so funny. His dad was right. I mean, Fadza had a Master's in Engineering from London, and he was a promising young man with a budding career as a consultant in a reputable firm. He wanted to throw that away to sell women's clothes on a website with his girlfriend? Any dad would be alarmed to hear this.

But well, as the wise Selena Gomez once said, the heart wants what it wants. I made sure not to influence Fadza in his decision and assured him that I can handle it without him. But Fadza was adamant. It was a scary moment for me when he handed in his resignation. *Is this the right decision?* Before this, we had split our risks. Now everything was dependent on FashionValet because we were putting all our eggs into one basket.

'Are you sure?' I asked Fadza.

He answered confidently, 'Yes.'

For the next few months, Fadza had to win back his dad because his dad was so disappointed with the decision. Fadza decided to write his own script, and my respect goes out to him, but still, in reality, it is not easy when your parents don't agree with your decision. It takes a lot of guts to follow your heart, and although his dad did not agree, Fadza never resented him. He was present at every family meal, he visited his dad often and cared for him, and when he finally could, he contributed financially to his parents.

Over the years, Fadza's dad changed his stance on FashionValet, and though he never says it, I think he is very proud of his son. He talks about Fadza a lot to his friends, he calls him often and seeks his advice, and he even buys from FashionValet to show us support. Bless him!

I guess it also helped that we popped out a few grandchildren for him.

I thought this story might help some of you out there who are at crossroads—whether to follow your dreams or to follow your parents' dreams. I am not advocating you go against your parents, but like my dad always says, you have to write your own script in life. It's your life, it's up to you to do what makes you happy. In almost all cases, parents just want to see their children happy. They will butt in every now and then because they fear the unknown and want to protect their children from harm/risk/unemployment/accidents/illness/sadness/the wrong spouse/eating bad food/choosing the wrong microwave—you name it. That's what parents do! Trust me, I've had twenty-five-year-olds who could not come to work because they felt unwell and their *moms* calling me to let me know, and parents coming in for their children's job interviews at FashionValet. There really is no other love like our parents' love.

But as much as we love our parents for their love, we need to also make our own decisions, because we are the only ones living with those decisions. If I listened to my mom now, I would be unemployed and living on her couch because she loves me and can't bear to see me go through entrepreneurial heartaches. 'Kesian anak Ma,' she would tell me, which means 'Pity my child', every time I would come home late from work. And I knew that if I told her I wanted to quit, she would protect me and just give me a big hug. So that's why you can't complain to your parents about everything. No matter how tired or stressed I am, I rarely tell my parents because I don't want them to be sad.

You gotta do what you gotta do and pray that your parents will come to terms with your decisions in life. Whether you make the right or wrong decision, you might hear their disappointment come up every now and then, but hey, parents nag. If it isn't nagging you about the bad decisions you made in life, they would be nagging you about something else, so might as well.

Our Love for Local Brands

Now that Fadza was in the picture full-time, we could do more around the office. I don't remember us having divisions in our role at that time in 2011. Everyone literally did everything; that's the culture of a startup. No one said, 'That's not my job'. Everyone rolled up their sleeves to tackle come what may. One second, Fadza would be shooting stock in the studio and rotating mannequins to take multiple angle shots, while I'd be labelling stock on the floor and Asma' would be packing orders that came in. The next hour, we'd rotate and everyone would be doing something else. It was fun and the best part of being in a startup.

At this point, it really felt like everyone loved us. Customers loved us. The media loved us. I think even Afandi started warming up to us. Designers and brands, too, loved us. Before FV had existed, local designers and brands were relatively unknown, with the exception of some big names. Generally, the trust in local brands was low—local brands were either unknown or labelled as lower quality. We took it upon ourselves to change this perception—it was FashionValet's mission to elevate the local fashion industry. When working with local designers and brands, we got to know them better. We saw with our own eyes how much love and passion they had for their work, and we felt with our own hands the product of this love whenever we received the stock. This was something we wanted to show the world. FashionValet featured these brands: we sent newsletters to customers about them, we wrote stories and articles about them, we talked to the media about them, we lived and breathed local brands.

On a personal level, I developed a lot of love for the local fashion industry and the individual brand owners. I had a voice on my personal blog, Facebook and then Instagram, so I used these to the max. Very quickly, my Topshop and Zara items got pushed to the back of the closet, and I saw myself wearing local brands daily, from head to toe. I would take daily OOTDs (Outfit of the Day)—or, as the Gen Z's now call it, 'Fit Check'—and post them while tagging each brand and a link to the website, so people could buy the items easily. It didn't feel like a job; FashionValet and I were truly, madly, deeply in love with local designers and brands, and they loved us too.

Maybe it was the underdog spirit that was high in us that made us feel stronger together. Whatever it was, it created a strong bond between FashionValet and the local fashion industry. We worked together on so many things—taking feedback from customers, going through the sales figures together, working on exclusive collections together, even looking for suppliers together. For the first two years, I was in-charge of sending monthly sales reports to all designers and brands on FashionValet, and I would go through them one by one, line by line, to give my recommendations to each of them—you should make more long sleeves, pink sells better, this collection did well, this collection did not do well, etc. Imagine doing that for 200 different accounts! I zoomed into each one and went in-depth, because I wanted them to grow. If they grew, FashionValet grew. If FashionValet grew, they grew.

When it came to the end of month, where we had to bank in the sales to each designer and brand, Fadza and I would write the cheques to them one by one. If there were 200 brands, we wrote 200 cheques—

by hand! And we would bring all these cheques to the deposit machines at the bank and process each transaction, one by one. We would split the stack of cheques between the two of us and take two machines, so it would be faster. If there was a queue behind us, our faces would be so red because we would be taking so long and the people behind us would sigh and sound so annoyed. But this was what we had to do— online banking was at an infant stage back then, so it was all still very manual! It took ages to make payments to all the designers and brands, not to mention being very careful to tally the amount on the report, on the cheque and at the deposit machine. But the two of us endured this every month—we stood there patiently, excited that the designers and brands would be receiving money in their accounts because they sold through FashionValet.

FashionValet wasn't a typical platform for transactions by vendors. The relationships were a lot deeper, and we found ourselves getting involved in everything from A to Z. It felt like we were a family in the local fashion industry. And it paid off. Suddenly, customers' hearts had greater trust in local brands, and they made space for us in their wardrobes. Customers started emailing that they were glad to have discovered brands A, B and C through FashionValet, they posted OOTD photos on their social media and hashtagged #FVOOTD, and they sent us kind and motivating emails telling us how proud they were of local designers and brands. That really made us feel like we were doing something bigger than ourselves. There was a purpose to FashionValet—a really good one that impacted the community.

Double and Triple Revenue Growth

As time went on, orders increased, brands increased, incoming stock increased. We knew we needed more structure, so we started hiring people to do more specialized roles. We hired someone to help with operations and stock, someone to do product uploads on the website, and someone to do marketing and customer service. Friends came to join the team as well and that made work a lot more fun. Even my best friends like Asma', Tasha, Alia, Kim and the longest Original Gangster

(OG) of them all was Marissa, who was there for ten years! I've known Marissa since I was six-years-old, and so I trusted her to care for this baby of mine. She came to do marketing and customer service, and spent a decade going through every up and down with us. I loved having friends join us because work never felt like work. We'd swing our chairs to face each other from time to time, asking, 'What do you want for lunch today?' To name each memory is impossible, but I think everyone who has lived a startup life before will know how much fun it is being small, nimble and surrounded by friends.

Things were going really well.

We were the first in Malaysia to house local brands under one roof online, so we received a lot of buzz. Even though our marketing was relatively small, our customer database grew beyond my blog and orders had started pouring in to such an extent that we were panicking because we had underestimated the packaging we needed. At some point, we had to ship items in plain bags because the FashionValet.net packaging we ordered had finished earlier than expected.

I was doing interviews every other week with the media, and it seemed like we were the darlings of the startup world in Malaysia. I think every publication wrote about us, which helped us a whole lot because we definitely did not have the funds to pay a PR firm to help us. I did TV interviews, magazine interviews, newspaper interviews, you name it. To English publications, to Malay publications, even to Chinese publications—I repeated the FashionValet story over and over again. When I wasn't being interviewed, I was slogging away in the office, steaming clothes, packing orders, replying to emails, answering the phone, meeting brands, processing new stock and uploading items to the website. Within two years, Asma' and I had signed on 200 brands, just the two of us, and looking back, I have no idea how we managed to do that in such a short period of time. After the second year, we no longer had to pursue brands—they were coming to us to ask if they could list on our website!

At this point of growth, we were growing 100 per cent in sales every year. The first month we launched, our sales were about RM 30,000. We had nothing to compare this to, so we had no idea if this was good or bad, but we sure felt like we had made it in life. At the end of the first year, we saw RM 720,000 in sales. The second year, RM 1.2 million. The third year, RM 3.2 million. The fourth year, RM 8.2 million. We were doubling and almost tripling year on year, and couldn't believe it ourselves. It just felt too good to be true.

Although things were going well, we were still careful about our cash. We kept things minimal. Instead of paint or wallpaper, we printed photos of each other and just covered the walls with them, so every morning we would come into the office and be reminded of all the good times. Instead of more furniture, we'd sit on the floor and organize stock and orders. Instead of models, we'd hire our friends; at some point after we graduated from mannequins. All the money we had in the bank, we would spend on things that would impact the customers and designers—better features on the site, nicer packaging and a little advertising. I still remember the first time we did paid advertising—it was on *Harper's Bazaar* Malaysia—a little pullout in one of their editions that cost us RM 10,000. We felt like this was the coolest ad ever and was going to tenfold our orders. It didn't, of course. It's marketing, not magic.

The office was constantly in action. We grew into a small team, and it was one of the best times of our lives. When your team is that small, the bond is undoubtedly stronger. We knew everyone's families, would stay after hours just for fun, had lunch together every day and ate from the same plate. It was truly like a family. We were having so much fun and everything was going so well with the business, not a single day felt like work—to any of us.

It was thrilling. The rush of adrenaline wiped away any exhaustion I felt. I mean, my friendship bracelet business was fun, but *this*! This was at a whole other level, this was *real*.

I remember being alone in the office, looking at the new stock from a brand that I had to do quality control (QC), label and measure. I was tired as it had been full-steam ahead since the moment the website had gone live. My hair was out of place, my mascara had run a mile, my body was sweaty after carrying boxes of stock. I sat on the red carpet and looked around the room. There was no other sound except the sound of our expensive air-conditioner blowing the plastic wrappers from the stock. Suddenly, a tear fell down my cheek. A happy tear, followed by its other happy tear friends. Gratitude filled my soul, and I was overwhelmed by what we had achieved so far. I thought about my family and blog readers who had supported me, I thought about brands that had taken a chance on me, I thought about my team, heck, I even thought about Afandi. I thought about my late grandmother, Opah, whom I wheeled around the office in her wheelchair when we first opened. She would have been so proud of all this.

I felt blessed. In that moment, I felt so blessed, truly and utterly blessed.

Chapter 3

Growing Competition

Things were going well.

So well, in fact, that we started to attract competitors.

I was really close to the brand owners on a personal level, so we would message each other often about work or simply to share news. One day, one of them sent me a message.

'V, I think you should know that a website approached us to join them. They want to do exactly the same as FashionValet,' she said.

I swear it felt like my heart stopped.

'Oh, what website is it?' I asked, calmly. Inside, not so calm.

'XXXX. Go and check them out,' she replied, (I honestly can't remember any more because there were so many back then, hence the XXXX).

I knew going into the entrepreneurship life that we could not be afraid of competitors. I'd been told multiple times that competitors will always be there and that we just have to be better every time. I knew that.

But when you hear about a competitor for the first time, it gives you all sorts of nervous knots in your tummy. In fact, if any entrepreneur says they do not feel anything when a competitor comes up, they are probably lying and just trying to look macho. Maybe over time, you handle competitor news better, but the first time, at least, it will feel like someone took your heart out.

I had to reply to her. Even though I was worried and dying to check out this new website, I had to reply to her. Do I act professional? Do I show my worry? Do I act cool? Who knows! There's no entrepreneurship manual for this.

'Oh, okay. Thanks for letting me know. Let me check them out,' I wrote back.

I opened our FashionValet group chat (at that time, it was just the six of us).

'Holy s***, we have a competitor. WE HAVE A COMPETITOR, GUYS!' I announced to the team, causing panic all around, including within myself.

An example of what *not* to do as a leader.

The brand owner messaged me again, a few minutes later, 'In case you're thinking that I'm going to join them, I'm not. I'm loyal to FashionValet and always will be.'

I wish there was a 'screenshot' function back then because that message warmed my heart and I felt like pasting it all over the office. In the midst of worrying and thinking we were doomed, her message was so reassuring and so kind. *We're going to be okay,* I thought, *we're going to be okay.*

Over the years, more competitors popped up. Some worried us, some didn't, but even the ones that worried us didn't last long. Even with their fancy features (one of them had VR feature, where you could measure your body with a camera function and they'd recommend the size. It was great, but in 2011, they were too early), their websites could not overtake FashionValet. It felt like we were untouchable, and there were several reasons for that. One, we had a one-year headstart, so we were already seen as the pioneers and leaders in retailing local brands. Two, the big brands had signed exclusively with us early on, so no other website could stock them. Three, the bond was strong between the brands and FashionValet, so it was very difficult for competitors to break that. Four, the brands trusted me. Having put a person's face to the brand helped us tremendously, and since I myself had a large personal following, it wouldn't make sense for them to move to a new website.

Every time a new competitor approached a brand, they would inform me. Together, we would go through these websites and their strengths and weaknesses. The team and I did not panic any more after a while; if anything, it just fuelled our fire to become better and better. Any feature they had that we didn't, we quickly worked to develop it. Any service they had that we didn't, we quickly worked to provide it. We were improving our own website constantly in order to stay ahead. My competitive nature would never let me be complacent, even till today. At the same time, we also felt reassured because (a) we had customers who came from among my loyal blog readers and (b) we had vendors who were more than just vendors to us. I was constantly getting messages from brand owners and designers that they were loyal to FashionValet and were not even thinking about joining the other websites. We were grateful for one another.

So far, so good. We really were on track to become the largest fashion website in Malaysia. With the support from the brands and designers, with the hardworking team and love from our customers and my followers, nothing could stand in our way.

Not true.

One fine day in 2011, I was in the office with Fadza. I was doing product uploads on the computer, and a message prompted.

'V, another website just approached us. They're from Germany, and they seem like a big company. You should probably look into them,' a message from one of the designers read.

Something in me sparked a worry that I'd never had before. I'd gotten used to competitors by now, but this one felt different.

'What is the website called?'

'Z something. I can't remember, I'll find it again and get back to you.'

The Big Z

She didn't need to. Ten other brands messaged me about this new website, soon after. Apparently, they had approached almost all of the brands on FashionValet already. I was annoyed. It felt like we had done all the hard work, and our brand list on the website had become but an easy reference for others to use for contacting them.

'I found it. The website is called Zalora,' she got back to me later, but by then, I already knew and was deep in research mode about them.

They were owned by Rocket Internet, a huge company in Germany that specializes in ecommerce. They had successful websites overseas and were now looking into expanding to the Asian market, one of the countries being Malaysia, of course. They were looking to house thousands of brands and were advertising on the job market, looking for so many different positions—some of which I never even knew existed. They had hundreds of millions in capital to inject here and were known to spend millions on just marketing budget alone. At that time, spending RM 10,000 dollars on marketing was something we would have to think about three or four times. So yeah, a *little* bit of a threat, I suppose.

For the first time, I saw a flash of worry on Fadza's face, too, which he hid quickly when he saw me looking at him reading an article about Rocket Internet coming to Malaysia. Articles were popping up everywhere in the media about them, and we were getting more and more messages from brands and designers that Zalora was trying to sign them on.

'Should we be worried?' I asked Fadza.

Fadza could never lie to me. 'I don't know,' was his honest answer.

We wanted 'no' to be the answer to that question, but we both knew that this wasn't like any competitor we had seen before. This new website called Zalora was going to be a threat to us, and we both knew it.

We both kept quiet for a while, each of us deep in thought about the future of FashionValet.

One week passed, and it was business as usual for us. We carried on as normal, but the worry was always at the back of our minds.

Suddenly, I got a message from Fadza.

'Zalora contacted me. They want to meet us,' it read.

What?

Why?

'We Want to Learn More'

'Okay, make sure you don't tell them everything, okay? They're a competitor!' I said to Fadza, all frazzled.

'I know, don't worry,' he replied.

This was in 2011, only a year after we had launched. We still had no idea why Zalora wanted to see us. Maybe they wanted to list our brands. Maybe they wanted to collaborate. Maybe they wanted to find out how we operated. Maybe they wanted to partner with us on something. Maybe they wanted to spy on us. Maybe they wanted to threaten Fadza and hypnotize him to reveal all our numbers. So clearly, guys, *clearly* I've been watching too many movies.

They probably saw us as a small fry in the industry, but to me at the time, they were Threat No. 1. Taking away business from us, wanting to lure all the brands and designers to switch over to them and gain the biggest market share. That was the reality of it all, so they were not very high on my to-befriend list. But Fadza being the better half of us, the calmer one, agreed to meet with them to gauge any possible synergy between us.

That hour he was with them felt like a year to me. I was anxious to know what they wanted to meet us for.

Finally, Fadza came back to the office and looked a little bit confused. He told me that he met two executives from Zalora and that they were very nice. They expressed an intention to learn more about the market. The conversation then carried on; basically, they wanted to know how we ran our business, about our deal with local brands, about our customer database, and asked how many orders we get in a day. Fadza played along and was careful about what he said.

As I expected, nothing else materialized from that meeting so it made me think that they were just fishing for insights and sussing out the competitive landscape. Not saying that they had this intention for sure, but it's not unheard of that the big guys meet the small guys under the pretext of 'we want to learn more', so you have to be careful what you share and what you don't.

After that, it was business as usual. Except, it was not the same. Designers started meeting up with Zalora buyers, and some would send courtesy messages to me along the lines of 'we are just going to listen to what they have to say, that's all'. I can't lie and say I wasn't hurt by this, and flashbacks of the same designers saying they will remain loyal to FashionValet kept playing in my mind. *How could they*, I naively thought back then, *after all we've been through growing together*. After all I'd personally done to promote them to my blog readers and followers. This was the first taste I had of the real world. The first lesson I learnt at the time—that 'business is business'; there is no loyalty because to a lot of people, it's just business, nothing personal.

Well, actually with human beings, it's always personal when we want it to be, and it's always business when we want it to be. Whatever is convenient for us to use at the time. It hurts, but it is what it is.

Slowly, I saw designers breaking our exclusivity clause and joining Zalora, either blatantly with their current brand name or creating a sub-brand as a loophole to the contract with FashionValet. They remained cordial with FashionValet, of course; after all we were still selling their items, and I was still personally wearing and promoting their clothes.

They were getting the best of both worlds as both platforms were fighting for them, and soon, we were playing with the rates. Whatever consignment rate FashionValet offered, Zalora would offer less. If we counter-offered a lower consignment rate, they would go even lower. Which designer would not want that lucrative offer? Who can blame the designers for switching?

So what could Fadza and I do? Match the rate and operate at a loss? How could we compete with this?

Dealing with Competition

First, never underestimate the power of relationships. As many as there were designers that moved from us, there were a lot that stayed loyal to us. They liked the focus that FashionValet had on local fashion, but my inkling tells me they also did not want to sever the relationship with me that we had built for years now. FashionValet had supported them and taken them on when they were unknown, so that bond was strong. They were pursued relentlessly by the aggressive Zalora buyers offering them extremely attractive rates, but they stayed on with FashionValet because they valued the relationship.

Second, we picked our battles. We knew we couldn't have everything. We let go of whichever designers and brands wanted to leave and instead put our focus on existing and newer brands on the site. But we fought for the designers and brands that we knew we couldn't lose, especially the established names that can bring in the traffic and sales from customers. Unfortunately for us, the more established the designer was, the bigger their demands were.

A bummer with that was that we had to play Zalora's game. If Zalora offered 20 per cent consignment rate, we would offer 18 per cent. If Zalora offers 15 per cent, we would offer 13 per cent. It did not make commercial sense for the business, but we were willing to take losses for certain designers in order to keep customers on our website. The designers were loving this, of course, as they gained from this rates war, but FashionValet was suffering. We were hoping that the sales we got from the rest of the brands would cover for the losses that we inherited from one or two established designers. Even when we 'won' the designer over Zalora, it wasn't a win. Every order sent out was at a loss.

There were a lot of moments when we felt really small. Constantly compared to a giant, how can you feel powerful? It didn't help that sometimes we were being strung along by some designers and brands (not all, of course). For example, while negotiating, they would tell us Zalora is offering them x per cent rate to get us to lower our rate, when in fact Zalora would not have offered them any rate at all. Negotiations become more difficult when a competitor comes into the picture, and this was the start of me losing that strong comrade spirit with the local fashion industry, because it was now all about 'what can FashionValet counter-offer me?'

One example I remember that left a mark was my business encounter with this one renowned fashion designer. Let's call her 'K'.

K was at her peak at the time, and we were proud to carry a preorder of her collection. We took a very low commission for it so every order was at a loss, but the weight that her name had on the website was worth it. I still remember a beautiful beaded jacket that I bought for myself from that collection. So many customers anticipated this launch and orders came pouring in.

After the success of this launch, we carried on working together. They were about to launch a collection of scarves, so of course, I fought to carry that launch on FashionValet. We negotiated some terms and came to an agreement. *Yes!* I announced to the team that a big launch was coming, and we got to work.

K's team came to the studio for the shoot of these scarves, and expressed their unhappiness over the equipment we had. 'This is our biggest designer,' I said at the time, 'buy whatever we need to buy to make them happy'. The studio team went to buy more equipment that evening itself and lugged them all back to the studio immediately; a new backdrop that her team wanted changed and some lighting that they wanted. We spent thousands, which we did not budget for, but it was needed to keep this brand on FashionValet. The entire next day, we did the photoshoot, and they were happy with the photos. Phew! Their team sent over the linesheet (a sheet containing product details, description, price etc.), and we uploaded each product one by one.

All the work was being done before the big launch. We prepared for the photoshoot, paid for all the models, prepared all the uploads on the website and the marketing team was readying all the banners and newsletters to blast to our customers.

I still remember what happened next.

I had just given birth to Daniel, my firstborn. It was the start of Ramadhan in 2013. I was doing my confinement in my parents' home. When Fadza came back that night, and as we were changing Daniel's diaper (a whole ordeal with a bowl of warm water and cotton buds, you know, first child . . .), I said to him, 'I feel uneasy, like something is not right.'

'How come?' Fadza asked.

'I don't know,' I answered honestly.

'Maybe you're just tired. Doctor says your body is still healing,' he comforted me. He propped up my feet on the bed and told me to rest while he looked after Daniel. *My sweet, sweet husband,* I sighed as I watched him.

In the middle of the night, I woke up because Daniel was crying. Breastfeeding duties—such is the life of a mother. While breastfeeding him, I decided to open my laptop to check the website. I do this often; I was obsessed (still am) with checking that things are in order or simply to check sales or emails.

I saw an email from K. I quickly opened it, in case there was something we had missed out so I could fix it myself there and then. I mean, the launch was soon!

Her email is now a blur to me, but in a nutshell, she wanted to personally inform us that she had decided to move her launch to 'another ecommerce website'. I had to read it twice because her words and tone were so nice, but basically it translated to 'I'm pulling out and giving this to your competitor, even though you've done all the work.'

Wait, was she serious? Was this email a prank? We had already agreed, and worse, we had done all the work necessary. I thought of the team. What was I supposed to tell them? What do I even reply to this email? She was cutting deals with another ecommerce website *while* we were working on her launch? Of course, negotiations would have to have happened days or weeks before. So while we were slogging away for her, she was meeting our competitor to get a better deal? And she couldn't even bring herself to call or text me, and had sent a formal email instead? I don't know if it was the postpartum hormones, but I felt my blood boiling.

A few days later, the collection launched on Zalora. I kept my cool in front of the team, but when they weren't looking, a tear fell down my cheek. At that time, I felt really small and like we had lost.

Looking back now, I knew it was 'just business, nothing personal'. At the end of the day, K had the right to choose whichever platform she wanted to be on. Of course, she could have chosen a nicer way to do it but on the bright side, we had upgraded our studio, and our photos from then on looked amazing.

This episode again reminded me of the realities of the business world, the sucky feeling of being 'the smaller guy' and most importantly, it taught me that everything must have a written agreement. No matter how much you like or trust someone, how nice the person is to you, there must always be a black-and-white document.

Chapter 4

Fundraising

Should We Raise Money?

Whether we liked it or not, our honeymoon period was over. Competition was getting tougher, brands were being poached and we would start losing customers soon. We needed more money for marketing, for operations, for recruitment, for equipment upgrade, everything!

There was one thing we could do.

Raise funds.

Fundraising was a scary word for me. When I hear fundraising, I picture people in suits, graphs on the board that go upwards, thick contracts and lots of jargon like RCPS, EBITDA, DCF and valuations. If I was an emoji, I would be that yellow one with its eyes popping out.

For first-time entrepreneurs like us, this was a new territory. Fadza and I both grew up looking at traditional family-owned businesses; there was no fundraising talk there. But this wasn't something we could pass on to anyone else in the company. The responsibility of keeping the company afloat was on the both of us. So even back in 2012, we started exploring the idea of fundraising.

First, we looked at getting loans. Of course, it was easier to take a loan, but no banks wanted to look at us because we were too new and did not yet have a profitable track record. That was such a bizarre concept to me. If I had lots of profits, I need you for what?

When we *did* get banks' interest, they would ask us for personal guarantees, i.e., if the company couldn't pay back the loan, Fadza and I would be personally liable to do so.

'What does that mean?' I asked the bankers.

'If the company can't pay the loan, you have to pay the loan. If you can't pay the loan, you will be declared bankrupt.'

Oh wow, okay . . . cool cool cool cool.

gulps

The only assets Fadza and I had were our healthy kidneys, and we doubted the banks wanted that.

As much as they wanted to help small businesses and young entrepreneurs, they had a lot of governance and rules, so they could not take big risks. That's just how banks everywhere work. Since banks were not an option, we had to find other ways. We could ask our family for loans, but we had vowed not to burden the family any more than we already had. If anything, we wanted to create FashionValet *to help* our families, not *ask* for help from them.

Second, we learnt of this thing called grants. We were told that there was a government body at the time called Cradle that gave out grants to help tech entrepreneurs. We were entrepreneurs, check! We were in ecommerce so it fell under the tech category, check! We went on their website to find out more, and we seemed to fulfil all the criteria for eligibility, so we emailed them to apply. They wanted to see our business plan, our sales projections, and current financials. We did this all for the first time by referencing templates on Google (God bless Google!). After a few weeks, we were selected for an interview. I remember going in nervous, with cold hands and shaky knees. We knew our business inside out, but four men in suits asking questions can be pretty intimidating. We swallowed our nerves in the end and answered all the questions they had.

'That went well,' Fadza said, as we both smiled, walking out.

'I think we got it,' I said in the lift, sincerely believing it.

Fadza and I thought we did pretty well during the interview. We had a clear business plan, we were an existing business already (not just an idea), and we were already doubling and tripling our growth, so there was a proven track record that FashionValet worked. Surely, we were promising contenders for the grant.

A few weeks later, we heard back from Cradle.

'Ahhh, today's the day. Bismillah!' I exclaimed, full of hope. Fadza was also smiling. We had asked for RM 500,000 and we already knew how to allocate this money for the business.

We opened the email, and we both kept quiet.

The email started, 'We regret to inform you . . .'

Our application had been rejected.

Their reason was that we were not innovative enough.

We accepted the decision because obviously no one can feel entitled to something they never had, but our spirits were crushed at the time. We were an ecommerce company that was *already* making money; they were a government body that *helped* tech companies. Did it not make sense that we thought we deserved the grant? Wouldn't we be the kind of companies that Malaysia would *want* to back? It made me wonder about the companies that actually received the grants. But alas, it wasn't up to us. We accepted our fate and thanked them for their time because we had to move on, with or without the grant.

The Last Option

So we had to explore a third option: getting investments from companies and venture capitalists. This one scared me because this was the most expensive form of fundraising. This was the fundraising in which you had to give a piece of your company away, like giving a piece of your baby away. We had given away stake before to my dad, but he's family. Giving it to strangers felt so alien.

I read articles about it to educate myself, but I still found it mindboggling in the early days of 2012. So you mean someone comes in to give you money to put into your business, and then you have to give them shares of your company . . . forever? So then the company is no longer fully yours. You have now invited other people you don't know into bed with you. You no longer have free reign to make whatever decisions, because now you have shareholders you need to consult and, depending on the contract terms, even ask for permission to do things. You have to ask for permission to do things with your own company?! This sounded like having extra parents, and it didn't sound very fun to me. What if they didn't agree with my decisions that I truly believed in?

People don't just give you free money. There's no such thing. You will have to promise them something in return. Giving them shares is a given, but you have to promise them something *more* to get their investment—sales targets, growth and, eventually, profits. And for some investors, there is even a clause that you have to give them shares *and* pay back the investment—it's meaner than a loan! So what happens if I don't hit my sales target? Will they sue me? What if I can't afford to pay out dividends? What if I didn't want to sell my company in the future, how will they exit and get returns on their investment? Then I'll have to buy back their shares. But with what money?

All these questions played in my mind, and rightly so. These are all difficult questions every entrepreneur has to think about when inviting an investor into the company.

We thought about it long and hard, spoke to a few people in the industry who had been there done that. At the end of the day, we were confident in our business, we had numbers to prove it and both of us were the ambitious type. There was no way but up. I could never see myself slowing down FashionValet; if anything, I want to ramp it up even faster. Whatever the investors' concerns were would already be our concerns, and the investors' goal of growing the company was already aligned with ours. We would be on the same page.

Fadza was already keen on fundraising; he was already two steps ahead of me. I was the more sentimental one between the two of us. I thought about the sleepless nights I stayed up to edit photos and the countless moments sitting on the floor folding clothes. This was our thing, our 'baby'. *Should we really get strangers into this?* That was the question on my mind in 2012.

There honestly is no right or wrong answer to that; it just really depends on your ambitions. If you want to grow a company big and fast, most likely, you will need outside investment; a boost of capital injected upfront for you to do a lot of things. If you want a profitable business that grows from your own cash flow, it will be smaller and slower growth but you won't have to take anyone's money or answer to anyone. It really depends on what you're comfortable with, and don't let anyone pressure you into doing one or the other. Do whatever feels right for you, and trust your own path and timing.

For us, we chose the former. We needed to survive, and we thought having an aggressive competitor with deep pockets would push us out of business if we didn't fundraise.

Our Very Own 'Shark Tank' Moment

As if a sign from above, we saw an advertisement about a reality TV show called *MyEG Make The Pitch*, that gave out investments to companies. The thought of fundraising was daunting enough, and this involved doing it on national television for everyone to see. If you win, great. If you lose, the whole country will be watching that failure.

In the end, we decided to just do it. The thought of not trying at all bothered me more than losing in public. Even if we lost, I thought, at least it would be free marketing on TV for FashionValet. We could not afford TV airtime at that time, so this was another way of getting on TV for free.

We got through the screening, beating many other companies.

Then we got through the first round.

Then we got to the semi-finals.

It was all happening so fast, and we were becoming one of the favourites that people were rooting for. So many people sent us words of encouragement. The video of us being grilled by the panel of judges is still on YouTube, much to my embarrassment. Till today, I cringe at how nervous I looked. I wore one of my favourite Radzuan Radziwill batik tops from FashionValet for good luck, and I keep it till today to remind me of that moment. Yes, I cringe, but seeing it also puts a smile on my face. As nervous as Fadza and I were, we were a couple of young ones braving the entrepreneurship world, putting ourselves out there on TV, vulnerable to everyone, just to fight for our dreams. Never mind the fact that we wanted to pee in our pants at that time; the fact remains that we powered through. I hope young entrepreneurs watching that will want to fight for their dreams, too, undeterred by the naysayers.

We got through the semi-finals and before the finals, every company was given a challenge. We were each given RM 5,000 and the challenge was to spend this in the best manner. We would be tested on creativity and sales.

At that time, we did what we thought was the smartest way forward. We did two things. First, we hired a video company, CelebrateTV, to do a brand video about FashionValet and posted it on all social media platforms. Second, we engaged our first-ever celebrity ambassador, Neelofa, who had just won the 'Dewi Remaja' competition at the time and was on the rise.

Our thought at that time was 'marketing, marketing, marketing'. Yes, people already knew of us from my following, but it wasn't enough. People needed to know what FashionValet actually *is* and see what it is we actually *do*, hence the video. It wasn't enough to show them the URL of a website. I have always believed in not just promoting products but more importantly, *telling* the brand story. We filmed in the office, showing everyone the entire process from how we shot the products to how we packed orders to how we wrote airway bills. Putting it on Facebook and YouTube meant that it gave us reach beyond my blog readers, available for anyone at all to watch and share with others. It had a lot of views, and it increased people's trust in and love for FashionValet, now that they saw us. After all, seeing is believing.

To support that, we wanted to show social validity. People needed to see other people using the brand. A celebrity endorsement can give the company more credibility, and via Neelofa, we hoped to reach her followers, especially those who did not know of FashionValet. Back then, influencer marketing was so much more effective (and cheaper).

Now the market is so saturated that every other post from every other person on Instagram is selling something to you, so the weight of one post is never like what it was before.

After one last session of interviews with the judges, we waited for our fate at the finals.

The day of the final interview arrived.

Was MyEG going to invest or not?

We felt confident, but after the Cradle episode, we never got our hopes too high. Anything could happen. *Win or lose, we have to move on,* we reminded each other.

Fadza walked back into the studio, where the four judges sat behind a panel. I was in a room on the set, watching live from a TV screen. He looked nervous; I knew he felt nervous. It was a RM 1,000,000 moment. Whatever came out from the judges' mouths was going to determine if we were going to receive a million bucks or not. How do you even put an emotion to that? It was a nerve-racking moment for the both of us; we were shaking!

'FashionValet,' the panel judge looked at Fadza, his eyes sharp and intimidating.

I was in the waiting room, watching on a small screen, because they only let one person from the company receive the verdict.

He continued, 'We would like to offer you RM 1,000,000 in return for 30 per cent of the company'.

The words sounded like music to our ears. I jumped up and down by myself in that room.

Finally, someone who believed in us and wanted to back us. Finally, someone who wanted to give us capital to grow the company. Finally, we could spend more on marketing. Finally, we could even buy stocks from established designers. Finally, we had a chance to fight on as entrepreneurs.

We celebrated for a while in the office, but then it was time to get back to some serious work. What you see on TV aren't the final terms. More negotiations usually happen off-camera, and in the end, we agreed to a deal. On signing day, I still remember going to their office and sitting at the conference table. Before me were stacks of documents for both Fadza and I to sign. It was scary, and I remember shaking while I signed. Mixed feelings of excitement, nostalgia, happiness, worry—all crept up, enveloping my entire body. For the first time in my life, I was sharing a piece of my 'baby' with a non-family member, and you can never really know if you're doing the right thing or not at the time. This is just the honest truth that I want you readers to know—that if you feel this way, it is completely normal and well . . . human.

The day that the investment money appeared in the company bank account, I think Fadza and I had to stare at the screen for a couple of minutes in silence. There were no more mixed feelings. We were committed and ready for the future.

Let's spend this investment, and surely, it would give us back ten times!

Boy, were we wrong. Not about our investor, but us.

We lost to temptation.

Keep reading.

Falling Prey to Temptation

We used part of that money to hire more people in the office. We could not cope with stock processing, product uploads and order fulfilments with the current team. At this time, everything was still manual, so it took a lot of labour of love.

The bulk of the money went into marketing. We saw that Zalora advertised everywhere and so many people knew about them. We learned the term 'guerilla marketing', which they were doing, the kind of marketing where you just spend a huge amount of money aggressively in all marketing channels together. Of course, you can only do this if you have millions in cash to burn. I would not recommend this. There are smarter ways to spend your marketing dollars.

But we were young and naïve. What did we know? If our competitor is doing it and they're so much bigger, it must be the right way.

So we splurged it all on digital marketing. Facebook ads, Google ads, YouTube ads. Burn, burn, burn. My marketing team now would laugh at how I was running our campaign back then. We had little knowledge of customer segmentation, awareness versus conversion ads, what kind of creatives we should put out, etc. All we knew was if you blast an ad online, it should get people to come to the website and spend.

Oh boy, were we wrong. We hardly saw any change in sales from the digital ads.

My frustration grew. I looked at the numbers daily, I monitored the ads like a hawk. I did everything that they were doing. Why was it not working? I soon realized that what worked for other competitors might not work for us, and that is actually a lesson I carry with myself until today.

For FashionValet, our story is the local brands' story. Not many would readily buy local fashion brands at the time, and we lost in variety to giant brands like Zara and H&M. Of course, things have changed tremendously in the last decade, but back then, local brands didn't have consistent ready-to-wear collections—most would go to local brands only for custom-made Eid outfits or wedding dresses. So for us to put up digital ads of FashionValet being just another ecommerce store was futile. The ads were too clinical; they were flat and impersonal, and I soon realized that the FashionValet story needed to be told differently. People needed to feel like they were contributing to a bigger purpose when shopping at FashionValet—the purpose of supporting local entrepreneurs, artisans and the people who poured a lot of love into their products. They needed to know that whenever they purchased a product on FashionValet, they made a local designer smile and that they were helping build the lives of us underdogs in the local fashion industry.

That investment was spent hastily, under pressure to compete with others, to whom we shouldn't even have been comparing ourselves. It was an expensive lesson that we learnt, and I hope I can help you dodge this mistake.

This was the temptation we lost to. We saw our competitor doing something and thought we should follow their strategy to compete with them.

Now that you've read this, I hope you'll remember to never be a slave to your temptations. Never be pressured to be like your competitor. Find your core, find your X-factor and double down on that. Don't try to be like someone else.

Getting More Attention

Despite all this, the business still went on. We didn't 10x our sales with that marketing investment, but at least the brand awareness had grown. Our popularity still grew. We were in the media a lot, and we were growing brands so fast that we even carried 500 local brands at one time.

Because of this, we received a lot of attention from investors. We received a lot of emails from venture capitalists wanting to invest in our company, and even individuals who wanted to be a part of our growth. Some looked legit, some didn't, so we were very careful in sharing any information.

The ones we took seriously were always the ones that were recommended by others we knew in the startup culture. In a world filled with sharks, we needed to hear testimonials and opinions from others so we could be reassured by their faith in certain investors.

One of the ones we took seriously was an investor from Silicon Valley. There happened to be a conference in Kuala Lumpur that year, which the government held to get investors into the country. We received some interest but pursued a conversation with this one particular investor more seriously than we did with others. After a lot of back-and-forth for months, we accepted their investment. It was purely a financial investment, but we thought having investors from Silicon Valley would help us greatly in learning their traits and scaling up fast. They were our first international investors and gave us a lot of global insight into what was happening in the ecommerce realm. We even travelled to Silicon Valley and visited the offices of Google, Facebook etc. via their connections.

That One Fateful Email

The business kept growing, and one day in 2015, we received an email from Japan. They were representing a Japanese ecommerce site and wanted to see if there was any potential partnership that we would like to explore. We had never thought of expanding to Japan; it didn't seem like our market. But there was no harm in talking, so we replied to their email asking for more information. They replied that they'd be in Kuala Lumpur the week after and were hoping they could visit our warehouse. *Umm, what?*

Fadza and I were discussing how to reply. They're strangers, why on earth should we let them come and see our operations? But what if they were legit investors who could propel our growth? We decided to just let them come to the office for a meeting (by this time, we had a standalone warehouse separate from the office), and from there, we would follow our gut feelings about them.

When the Japanese guys came to the office, we instantly felt comfortable. They presented their company, and we presented ours. They explained that they wanted to expand into Southeast Asia and invest in existing businesses instead of building their own from scratch. For Malaysia, FashionValet came highly recommended to them. Nawww, stahhhp.

'Eight million ringgit. That's very good, very good,' they said in their Japanese accent, as they nodded politely, looking at our sales numbers from 2014.

I was beaming with pride.

'Thank you, we try to work hard around here. May we know your revenue?' I asked.

'Sure, sure,' the chief financial officer said as he took out his calculator. He pressed some numbers to convert the currency and finally said in a small voice, '1.2 billion dollars'.

Maybe I had heard wrong.

'I'm sorry, what did you say?' I asked.

He looked taken aback and discussed with his Japanese colleague next to him, to check if it was wrong. They calculated again to confirm and said, 'Yes, correct, 1.2 billion dollars.'

I almost fell off my chair. These guys were running a billion-dollar company, and they were sitting in *our* meeting room, breathing the same air as us?

'Malaysian Ringgit?' Fadza asked.

'US Dollars,' they replied, looking down, almost ashamed to tell us. OH MY GOD, THEY WERE BILLIONAIRES!

What do we do when we meet billionaires?

Do we . . . do we bow?

Do I, like, bow right now?

I didn't know how to react. It was so cool that they were running such a big ecommerce business, and I was desperate to learn everything I could from them. Here we were, gloating about our tiny million in front of them. They didn't even talk in millions any more; they spelt million with a B!

We went to the warehouse, and I'm glad Fadza and I followed our gut feelings. It turned out to be such a helpful warehouse visit because they pointed out so many things we could improve on, from little things like what baskets to use when segregating orders, to inventory management systems. In just an hour with them, we learnt so much about operations enhancements. Imagine what more we could do if they were a part of us!

It turned out that they were the largest fashion ecommerce company in Japan. After that visit, Fadza and I had only one wish. Please, please, let this Japanese investment go through. And it did. It turned out they liked us a lot too, both the business and the founders. *changes status to 'In A Relationship'*

This investment wasn't just a financial one for us; it was strategic, too. We wanted to learn how to manage operations as we scaled and how we, too, could grow to a billion dollars. US dollars, please.

Since the investment, they've helped us beef up our operations— the backend parts that customers don't see. It got difficult to learn via email and video calls wouldn't work because most of their employees didn't speak English, so we decided making a trip to their office in Japan would be an amazing opportunity to learn. Which billion-dollar ecommerce company would open their doors to anyone? It's because we were their investee company that they more than welcomed the sharing of knowledge.

That trip to Japan was *mind-blowing*. We were brought to their office first and had an introductory meeting in their conference room. There was a beautiful wooden table, a big fat solid one.

'Beautiful table,' I said as I placed my bag on it.

'Thank you. This was bought by our founder. I think it was a million dollars,' they said nonchalantly.

Gulp.

I immediately lifted my bag and put it on the floor. There was no way I was going to risk scratching that table with anything. After that, I was scared to even sit on the chair, which probably cost a hundred thousand dollars or something.

After the welcome meeting, they gave us a tour of their warehouse. We had to drive further into the town, and we finally saw that beast of a multi-storey building. Their warehouse was called ZOZOBASE, a mini-town in itself that had everything from a cafeteria to loading bays to a warehouse to their fulfilment centre. Each floor served a different purpose—some were for inventory, some were for QC, some were for fulfilment. Everything was automated and computerized, and their employees worked so efficiently. Discipline was definitely a value there because all employees went for lunch at a certain time; they even had breaks to wash hands. They moved so seamlessly and everyone was so focused on their tasks. Everything was so neat, and the floors were so clean that I'm pretty sure I could roll around on it and lick it. There were conveyor belts in the order-sorting area, and I stood there for a good few minutes, just observing. This was my dream come true.

At that time, we were having issues with our studio back home. My team brought up the issue of needing more stylists, more photo editors and photographers. So I wanted to see how they ran their photoshoots here. My jaw dropped when I saw it. There were small booths, with railings on both sides (one for the 'to shoot' pile and another for the 'done' pile). There was no photographer. There was just a model. She changed into a top, posed in front of the camera for two seconds, changed into another top and posed again. It all happened so fast and she managed to shoot so many items in just five minutes.

'Where is the photographer?' I asked them.

'Oh the model takes their own photos. They hold a small device in their hands, and just press it to take photos when they pose. Then the photos go straight out to the editing team.'

What . . .?

It was so efficient that I wished my whole team could see this. We were not allowed to take photos or videos, so I refrained, but man, I was dying to break that rule.

That trip alone opened our eyes to the possibilities ahead. It made us see how big we could become, and how small we were at the moment. It showed us the potential and fuelled our motivation to want to grow even more.

So that's the power of having a strategic investor versus a purely financial one.

To Get Investment Or Not to Get Investment?

That is a question only you can answer for yourself.

For us, we had a few more rounds of investments into the company, including by Khazanah and Permodalan Nasional Berhad (PNB). We were very proud to have Malaysian funds backing us; after all, we were a proud Malaysian company growing Malaysian brands.

Contrary to what some might believe, I never had any connections or a 'backdoor' to these investors. I networked a lot to broaden my reach in the entrepreneurship field, I attended conferences and business events, so I grew my name and credibility in the business world organically. I was never handed any investor on a silver plate; there is no such thing. There is no investor who would invest in a company they don't believe in. So yes, Fadza and I had to go through rounds of meeting multiple investors, getting multiple rejections and scoring a few good ones along the way. Fundraising is a tiring journey, but the more pitches you make, the better you get at it.

I have to admit that once you start fundraising, there is this desire to keep on fundraising. It becomes a valuation game, wanting to drive up your valuation and taking a lot of pride in that. We were valued as high as USD 100 million very early on in our journey and that does a lot for your ego. We got sucked into the game, and after a while, our sales projections became harder and harder to achieve.

We were forcing the company to grow in order to hit our targets to satisfy investors, but if you grow too fast, things can go really wrong.

Have you seen WeCrashed on Apple TV? It's a show about the co-working space company WeWork started by husband–wife founders that got valued at USD 47 billion, and it is one of my favourite series ever, because it's so bizarre yet so relatable—the story of passionate founders that started a business and got lost in the pursuit of big dreams and high valuations. Fundraising can be dangerous because it can mask a lot of things that are going wrong with the fundamentals of the business. When you don't have enough money, you fundraise, then you soon finish that money quickly, then you fundraise again and again. You never stop to check if there are serious problems with the business model or with the product itself, or any problem at all that needs fixing, because your solution is to just throw more money at the business. In the end, the bubble will burst, and your business will crash.

At the end of the day, you need to take a pause and really ask yourself why you are accepting investments into the company. Is it the right time? Is it the right amount? Are you being pressured by a competitor? Is it for fame and glory, or do you really need the money? Can you get the money from elsewhere?

And once you're sure you are ready for an investor, ask questions about them. What have they invested in before? Who are the people behind the funds? What are their expectations from your business? How long do they want to invest for? In what year do they have to exit? Apart from money, is there anything else you can benefit from through this investor? Knowhows? Network? Retail connections?

Then, ask the awkward questions about worst-case scenarios. What happens if you don't hit sales targets? What happens if you change plans along the way? What happens if you fail? Do you have to pay them back?

These are all questions Fadza and I didn't think about in the beginning. Having a good lawyer who advises you on these things is crucial because a lot of hidden loopholes can be found in contracts. Getting a bad investor is something you have to live with for life, because once you let someone into your home, it's hard to get them to leave if things go sour between the parties. Some companies collapse because of investor disputes, and that brings shame to the business.

You may feel, at times, that you just need money to grow, but sometimes money is not the answer. There are companies with so much money that go bust, and companies with little money that really scale up. There is no wrong or right way, and more often than not, your gut feeling can guide you best.

All I can advise is that if you *do* want to raise money, do it when things are on the rise, when things are going well in the company. Fundraising is a long process and could take anywhere from six months to maybe even years. So if you start the fundraising process when you *already* need money, you will find yourself in a desperate state to accept whatever offer is given to you—even bad offers or offers with extremely low valuations. Plan ahead on your fundraising journey as much as you can.

Chapter 5

Growing Pains

'I need to go back to the office on the way home. I left something,' Fadza told me when we were at a *GLAM* magazine dinner event in 2011.

'Okay, sure,' I said, thinking nothing of it.

This was in the pre-marriage days, the days when I was able to drag Fadza to fashion events. Ah, those good old dating days when the guy just listens and says yes to everything.

It was important for me to attend fashion events, and FashionValet was a hot invitee for local brands because we were potential stockists. If anyone spotted me or any FashionValet buyer at a fashion event, they immediately expected the brand to be on the website soon after. I used to attend almost all events, which had taken a toll on my personal life. I had no personal life, everything was about work. As 'social' as these events were, it was still work. I approached people to say hi, I collected name cards and phone numbers, I participated in conversations, I was never shy to network.

I took every opportunity to mingle and meet people, which helped expand my network in the fashion industry *tremendously*. A lot of things can bloom from relationships with people, so as an entrepreneur, you must come out of your comfort zone and meet as many people as possible. This is not something you should delegate to other people in the company, *you* must do it the most.

After half an hour at the event, Fadza asked his favourite question, 'Can we leave soon?'

There was a designer I had spotted at the other side of the room. I couldn't leave the event without talking to her. 'Just a few minutes more, okay?'

A few minutes became half an hour, and Fadza kept looking at his watch.

I knew I should have brought Asma' instead, I thought.

'Okay, okay, let's go,' I finally said.

More Than Just an Office

On the way to send me home to my parents like a gentleman, Fadza reminded me that he needed to stop by the office. The office then was two minutes away from my parents' house, so it was convenient. All of us were always going in and out of the office so this was nothing out of the ordinary.

He parked in front of the office and opened the door. As he walked out, he asked, 'Aren't you coming?'

'No, it's okay. I'll just wait in the car while you run up.'

He looked around the empty parking lot. It was dark and scary. 'No way, it's night time. Anything can happen out here. Come with me, I'll just be a minute.'

'Okay, fine.' I walked up the stairs of the office with him, slightly annoyed that I had to accompany him. My dress was puffy, and I had a train at the back so I had to bunch it up and carry it as I walked. My feet were hurting so bad with blisters from the high heels I had on. Things men never understand.

He unlocked the front door and swung the door open. The office was pitch-dark except for one area. The lounge room was lit.

'Oh my god, did someone break in?' I panicked.

Oh my god, our stocks!

What if someone stole our entire inventory—oh, wait a minute . . .

We inched closer to the room, and my jaw dropped.

Before my eyes were candles everywhere. Flowers, too. On the shelves were photos of Fadza and I, our memories from London days all the way till now. I looked up at the ceiling, and there were photos hung from the ceiling too. Everywhere I looked, love filled the room. I looked at Fadza, and he grinned from ear to ear.

My heart skipped a beat.

He walked over to a chair and picked up a small box.

Oh my god.

Then he got down on one knee.

Oh my god. If this is a prank and inside that box is a keychain or something, I swear I will leave him.

He opened the box and in it lay a beautiful diamond ring.

'Vivy Sofinas Yusof, will you marry me?'

My heart skipped a beat. The love of my life was proposing to me, on the very grounds where we had poured our heart and soul to build our dreams.

I was over the moon and wanted to scream YES, but I responded with a more important question.

'Have you asked my dad?' I said, spoiling the moment.

Of course, I said yes! And right after that, from out of nowhere, all the girls in the office came out from the fitting room inside the lounge and ambushed us, shouting and screaming in celebration. My sister, my best friends, my colleagues. They had been hiding in that room the whole entire time. Of course. I wouldn't expect any less from them. #noboundaries

And that's the story of how Fadza proposed to me . . . in the office, with uninvited attendees.

The first FashionValet office means so much to me, not just because of the business. It was also special to me because so many of life's milestones and memories were made there, one of them being this proposal. It was so much more than an office. FashionValet wasn't just a place with files and stock, it was a place full of life and meaning for us. For all of us. In the journey, we met colleagues that became family, we saw each other get married, we saw each other becoming parents, we saw each other grow up and build lives. We saw each other grow in our careers too—we had someone who came in as an intern and after years is now rocking it as the Head of Operations of the Group. #HiSyiks! Even today, I drive past that office and smile, reminiscing all the good times.

Months followed, and in June 2012, I became Mrs Fadza. I married the love of my life and we even invited a few FashionValet customers to the wedding. My parents were the happiest and most relieved because they could finally stop spying on us in the office. A lot of the times, Fadza and I could not believe how blessed we were. We had a happy marriage, happy business, and everything was going so well.

For a while, at least.

Always Go with a .com Domain

'Gah, why do they always say our website is FashionValet.com?' I asked, as I put the newspaper down.

We were being featured in a newspaper positioning us as this new and hip local brands hub. It was a huge two-page spread, which was a fantastic opportunity for us to reach millions of Malaysians. Except that they would all be reading the article and then typing www.fashionvalet.com in the URL box, which would lead them to that drycleaning website in the US. Our website was www.fashionvalet.net! Just like that, we would have lost potential customers, with no way to get them back.

Remember when we thought it would be cool to be different and be FashionValet.net?

Not so cool after all.

Having a .net domain made it difficult, because automatically, when people think of a website, it has got to be a .com. Naturally, when people heard of FashionValet and were curious to check us out, they would type www.fashionvalet.com.

We contacted the owner of the domain (if I'm not mistaken, via an email address on the website) and asked if we could buy the domain from him. Turns out, the drycleaning business wasn't real—it was just a front. He replied and said he would sell the domain URL for '100,000 dollars'. US dollars.

'What?!' I exclaimed in disbelief. 'All this guy did was buy the domain and suddenly wants to sell it for a hundred grand?'

I found out then that this was an occupation for some people, to buy domains, do nothing with it and sell them to interested parties for a lucrative profit. Literally, you'd be sitting at home clicking some buttons and getting a handsome amount of money for close to no effort. I'm *kind* of jealous I didn't think of it first.

We obviously could not afford to spend USD 100,000 (RM 400,000) on a domain. At the same time, we couldn't go on with a .net domain if we wanted to scale. Changing our name to another available .com domain was not an option because we had already built the FashionValet name by then.

We needed to negotiate. We decided to go the soft route. We wrote back saying we were just a couple of young kids starting our business, didn't have much money and could not afford a hundred grand. We asked for his understanding and kindness, and we offered him USD 5,000 for the domain.

He agreed to sell to us at USD 10,000. It was a take-it-or-leave-it offer, so we agreed. Finally www.fashionvalet.com was ours.

The .net era ended, and so did the confusion by media and customers.

So guys, always go with a .com domain.

A *Very* Manual Process

I wished for what every entrepreneur wishes for; a fairy godmother to come and set up the backend systems and processes for us.

Typically, the entrepreneurs are the dreamers of the business. The visionaries, the ones with the big picture and creative minds. What I knew I wasn't was an operations and processes kind of entrepreneur. I hated structure. I felt suffocated by it and felt it slowed down the business. Of course, every business needs structure, though, so really, running a business brings a dreamer back down to earth. Whether you like it or not, you'll be the one setting up the filing system, designing the invoices, setting up report templates and creating the standard operating procedures (SOPs) for every single thing in the company. Every. Single. Thing.

From the moment we receive stock, we have to do up a stocklist signed by the brands and us for acknowledgement, to avoid inventory discrepancy. Then we have to sort and label each item, measure them and do QC. During QC, we lay out each item and check for stains, tears, loose threads, etc. We even have to do smelling tests to make sure they haven't been worn before. Yes, I smelled those armpits!

We take out one piece of each design and arrange them at the studio, ready for the catalogue shoot. Each product then undergoes a photoshoot (in the initial days, this was with the mannequin, whom we'd named Julie), with multiple angles and closeup detail shots. These photos are then uploaded to a computer and edited for colour correction because the flash sometimes distorts the colour. Back then, we used Julie every day, so she was chipping off in places and all that had to be edited out too (soon, we started using our friends as models because it was so much faster #andtheywerefree). Edited photos are then resized and uploaded together with product description, product code, measurements, etc.

On the launch day, we publish each product on the website for the customer to see. While we wait for the orders to come in, the stocks are kept in racks, waiting eagerly to be picked up and packed into parcels.

Once the order comes in, the order summaries are displayed. I wanted customers to receive nice and professional order summaries so I designed a receipt on Word document with our logo at the top. There were blank rows for name, order ID, address, phone number, email address and items bought, which were then broken into item name, brand name and product code. To make it even more complicated, I decided to add a running receipt number as well, because the order IDs did not necessarily match the sequence in which the order had been processed. We would get the order summary in the backend and copy-paste each line to fit into my beautiful Order Summary document that we would print two copies of, one for the customer and one for our filing. We waited patiently as the printer printed them, going zzzz zzzzz zzzzz as it paused for every line. That printer single-handedly taught me patience in life.

I was so excited to do our filing system as I watch them do in every movie that shows an office scene—with thick files that have months printed on the sides. The fatter the file, the better the business, I thought. So I would put all these order summary sheets into the file, separated by months.

Are you still there?

Just checking.

Then, we'd take one of each order sheet into the stockroom to do our picking. We couldn't cope with our hands (and top of heads) as orders increased, so we bought a trolley to collect all the ordered items. We matched the items to the order. The items were stacked on top of the order sheet, so if a customer ordered more than three items, the stack would fall off and spill into another order. The sheets of paper would also fly off whenever the fan blew, which meant we had to start all over again and curse whoever turned on the fan.

We would also match orders wrongly because there were two copies of sheet per order so sometimes they got mixed up, and customers would get a completely different order. There were countless times Fadza had to drive to pick up the parcel from Customer A's home, send it to Customer B's home and take Customer B's parcel to drive back to Customer A's home. We were mostly known just in Klang Valley in the beginning, so it was manageable, but one day, we sent the wrong order to a customer in Singapore, and we all gulped. Thankfully, one of our colleagues was going to Singapore that weekend so she lugged the parcel along and met our customer there. The customer was so understanding of our mistake, but still, it was embarrassing on our part!

We also wrote the Poslaju airway bills by hand. In the 'sender' section would be our company name, company address and phone number. We wrote all this by hand, until we grew some brains to order a company chop that we could just press onto the bill. Well, we had to press four times, actually, because each airway bill had four copies, but it sure was better than writing. In the 'recipient' box would be the customer name, address and phone number. Everyone raced to write airway bills for the orders with the shortest customer name. 'Ili', 'Jo', 'Lisa' were among our favourites. The full names with Sharifah something something Binti Syed something something were the most painful, and they would always leave those to poor old me to write, because I was the fastest writer among the lot.

One day, a parcel arrived at the office, and I examined the airway bill.

'Whoa!' I exclaimed.

'What?' Fadza asked, coming to me.

'This airway bill has our address printed on it, not handwritten,' I pointed out. This sender didn't sit and write each address on the airway bill, he just printed them #likeabawse.

Thanks to that parcel, we found out there was such a thing as an airway bill printer machine. And so we quickly bought one to help us become less manual and give our tired wrists a break. From then on, we no longer had to write on airway bills.

Once the airway bills were stuffed into each FashionValet postage bag, Fadza and I would load them all in Fadza's car and drive to the Poslaju centre. At Poslaju, we would hand them in one by one to the staff and wait for him to weigh each parcel to write down the weight. Then he would tear each airway bill for us to have a copy of the tracking number.

Fadza and I would split the airway bill stack in half (he took one half and I took the other half), and we'd go home and email each customer their tracking number, written on the airway bills. We had an email template but we had to type out each number and letter for every new email. And these tracking numbers are not A1 or something kind like that. More like MY12365ISTHISNECESSARY0371013847TYE. Okay, I'm exaggerating, but it sure felt like that! If we had a hundred orders, that would be a hundred manual emails sent.

So that's it, our very simple process at FashionValet!

Would you like to apply for a job here?

So much of what I wrote in here would be foreign to you and you're probably thinking, 'Why so stupid?' Again, this was back when automation was either unheard of, expensive, or not easy to do. The systems we had back then were as such, so we had to go through such a lot of growing pains. Now there are readymade systems where people can just click a button to do all these things. #slightlybitter

It was a *terrible* process that we had designed when we started in 2010. As twenty-two-year-olds who had never done this before, we just did whatever made sense to us with the limited knowledge that we had of machines and systems. Surprisingly, we got by with this for a good couple of years! The business was growing so fast that Fadza and I had no time to look at process improvements, so by the time we wanted to review processes, they had grown into a full-blown nightmare.

So to new entrepreneurs out there, automate whatever you can automate from the beginning. Human beings make errors, no matter how detail-oriented they are, so it's best to lessen the manual effort as much as possible. Over the years, with the help of our tech team, we automated almost everything, and as our volume increased to a decent level, couriers cared enough to do pickups so we no longer had to drive every day to the fulfilment centres.

Also, don't buy the cheapest printer in the shop, please. I can't tell you how many times I wanted to smash it with a hammer.

Should Have Taken an Engineering Degree

And that was just the processes. We also had to look at improvements on the website.

When we launched, we were in a rush. Remember I told you I was harassing Afandi and offering to work in his office to help him? Well, hurry makes bad curry, like my dad always says.

The website launched with the bare minimum. We worked off an existing template so it just had a menu bar, basic categories, photos, description, price, checkout—that's it. There were no size/colour/price filters for customers, no subcategories, e.g., shirt, long sleeve, short sleeve, etc. under Tops, no one-page checkout, no 'Add to Wishlist', no fancy features at all.

Looking back, I'm not sure if I would have changed anything in this area, though. Had we launched later, we would not have been the first multi-label fashion website in Malaysia. We might have had a nicer website to start with, but it would still require improvements along the way anyway. You would not know until you start listening to customers what features they wanted and what didn't really matter to them. No website launches absolutely perfect on Day One.

Over the years, we added more features based on customer feedback. Filters, size recommendations, subcategories, chatbox, image search and many more. I loved that I shared my story quite personally from the start because it felt like the customers were rooting for us; they were looking out for us, pulling us up higher at all times. Apart from a few angry demands that sprouted from a bad experience on our site, most customers were kind and forgiving whenever we made a mistake or lacked something. It was always an email that said, 'Please tell Vivy that she and team are doing a great job, but I want to suggest you add xxx and xxx on the website' or an email that ended with, 'It's okay, you guys will get there!' We wanted to deliver the best to our customers, but they understood that it doesn't happen overnight.

Throughout my ten-year journey in ecommerce, till today, I'm amused by the complicated jargon and steps that any tech team endures for even a small, teeny-weeny enhancement on the website.

I remember asking Afandi for subcategories.

It's literally adding another filter in the backend that my team can tick that says, 'Top—Shirts' or 'Top—Sleeveless'. Right?

Afandi laughed. 'No, Miss Vivy. If you want a subcategory, we will have to add this thing that will affect this thing and that thing. And we will have to do testing that will shut down the website for a few hours, and maybe even a whole day if there are errors. And then that thing might skew this, and the overall alignment on the website will skew. Also you'll have to do a drop-down menu here, and over there you'll have to adjust that column and this column. And that will affect this and that, and that and this.'

cricket sound

I can already picture my tech team reading this. Their eyebrows furrowing, deep in thought thinking about this process, nodding in agreement to whatever Afandi just said. 'Yes, he's right, that makes sense,' they are whispering right this second.

Me, on the other hand—still blinking.

I just wanted subcategories, man.

Tops—Shirts. Tops—Sleeveless.

That's all.

How did it get so complicated?

Literally, this is the conversation I had to go through whenever I asked for features. Not only does each process sound so complicated, the tech team also knows to add words like 'cache' and 'cookies' to distract me to think about Famous Amos. How can tech sound so delicious yet drive me crazy? Even simple enhancements are not as simple as us laymen think. To me, subcategories are just extra lines on the website that can give my customers a better experience. To tech engineers, it's a long document of action plans and testings. But because they are the experts, you have to trust them and make an effort to understand the processes they have to go through.

Each enhancement involves development at the frontend as well as the backend, and depending how big you are, it might affect other operating systems that are all linked together. So in the beginning, you have to pick and choose the features you want to prioritize because a lot of time and resources are required. Plus, tech enhancements ain't cheap! Every single improvement cost us thousands before we had our own in-house tech team.

Then there was the backend system.

While frontend is the website that the customer sees, the backend is what the team sees. We had a backend that we did everything on, e.g., managing orders, uploading products, adding subcategories (after like a year . . .), managing coupon codes for promotions, numbering each product so they show up in sequence on the website, among many other functions.

The numbering feature was hilarious. We had to put a number to each product, because if we didn't, the products would not come out in sequence. They would be sorted randomly, and when our customers clicked 'What's New', everything would be all over the place. New items could be on the last page, and old items could show up first.

So we numbered each product to put them in sequence. If the product was numbered as 1, the product would show on top. The product numbered as 2 would be the next one the customer saw. And so on. If the number was bigger, it would be on the back pages. So when we started, I said, 'Okay, let's just start with the first product we upload with the number 10,000 and go backwards,' thinking 10,000 was such a big number. Another one of my genius decisions as an entrepreneur, not thinking ahead. We got to 10,000 products in no time, and I thought uh-oh, the number was reaching 1 now. What happens after 1?

My content executive at that time, Rus, glared at me. 'Does this mean we have to *renumber 10,000 products* to numbers with more zeros?' Oh, if her looks could kill. She's been through all of these painful episodes that nothing, and I mean nothing, fazes her any more. Not even childbirth without an epidural. *We* made her tough, really.

At that time, there was no automated fancy-schmancy algorithm system or at least it wasn't widely available to all. Everything was manual, and it was painful. I was doing the calculations of renumbering the entire SKU inventory. There were like six of us at that time, so if we each took an average of 1,600 SKU, and we worked hard to renumber 100 a day, we could do this renumbering project in sixteen days. I gulped at the thought of telling the team this.

So, I tried something myself. What if I added a minus in front of the number so it became –1, –2, –3 and so on. If this worked, there would be no limit to the number of products because we could have a product with the number –465,723 and it would still be sorted in sequence.

I clicked on one of the older products and experimented. I added minus in front of its number. If this product became the first product on the website, that would mean it worked and I wouldn't have a problem any more.

I clicked 'Publish'.

I refreshed the website. *Please appear first, please appear first.*

It worked!

There it was. That product came first, and I breathed a huge sigh of relief. Crisis averted. We had products with negative numbering, which was ridiculous, but at least Rus liked me again.

The backend was the heart of our operations. In just one URL lay the whole company operations and data that we referred to. There was no backup, so if something went wrong, we were screwed. As we kept adding more features to the website, the backend got so much heavier that it slowed down our operations. Whenever the website had high traffic, not only could we not open the frontend, we also could not open the backend. That happened more often as the business got bigger and more popular, so it became a real problem. Whenever the website was down, we could not fulfil orders, we could not upload products, and we could not email customers.

We didn't have a floor of tech guys here—couldn't afford them. I looked at Rus, Rus looked at Fadza, Fadza looked at me. Fadza would email the server company, and we would wait . . . and wait. We were paralysed until the server company decided to reply to our emails (all ten of them with subject 'HELP' with exclamation marks). We'd had server companies abroad before, so it was even worse if there was a huge time difference. Here we were, panicking that our fort was collapsing and we were being flooded by angry customer emails, and on the other side of the world, the people who could fix our problems were sound asleep. Back then, third-party companies refused to give personal phone numbers so there was no way to reach them after office hours. I remember one day when we had a big launch and this happened for the umpteenth time, I went to the bathroom and started crying. Angry messages were pouring in, emails to which I had no idea what to reply, and even mean comments on my blog telling me I should just shut down if I didn't know how to run a website. I felt so helpless because I couldn't do anything but wait and kick myself for not having an engineering degree.

LAW. DEGREE. FOR. WHAT?!

We knew we had to fix this once and for all, but we had no knowledge of tech to even know the root cause of all these problems.

So we decided it was crucial to hire an in-house tech team. Tech talent is scarce in Malaysia, so it was definitely a challenge. Slowly but surely, we got there over the years and rebuilt the *entire* system from scratch because it was so messed up—this could not have happened had we not raised funds.

With the injections of capital from investors I wrote about in the previous chapter, we could do so much more. We could afford to hire a bigger team, hold fashion show events, join bazaars, engage more ambassadors, upgrade our equipment. The biggest chunk went into technology enhancements.

The outside world did not know of these hiccups we faced internally caused by our poor processes and operations. I put on a brave face every time I did an interview or spoke to external parties, so it was as if everything was going well with FashionValet. Thankfully, sales still continued to climb, and orders were pouring out of our doors daily. Externally, we were good, but internally, we had a lot of problems. As we worked over the years to fix our operational issues by bringing in experts, internal capacity started to catch up to external demand, and things started looking good again.

But like I always say, entrepreneurship is a rollercoaster ride. When there is good news, bad news will follow, which is then followed by some other good news. It's like getting a daily dose of heart exercises, so entrepreneurship is definitely not for the faint-hearted. We were just about ready to scale up—processes had been smoothened, technology improvements were ongoing, making us better and better.

Little did we know that soon, we were about to encounter the biggest challenge for FashionValet—the business model itself.

No Stock Means No Sales

'What do you mean they won't give us restock?' I asked the buying team.

'They said they don't have any more of that design.'

I went to the brand's Instagram account. 'Popular design restocked! Come to our store now!' the latest post said. *But they* have *stock!*

This was a growing dilemma at FashionValet. We would launch a brand on FashionValet with a collection. We would market the brand, promote their designs on our social media, send newsletters to all our customers that the brand is coming soon and spend on ads to market their brand. We would send them out to influencers to create buzz about this brand, and I would promote it as well on my personal social media accounts. We would join bazaars, too, and stand for hours educating people about local brands. For any new brand at the time, joining FashionValet was a stepping stone to getting their name out there.

But we started seeing the trend that brands would happily send stock the first couple of times, then send lesser and lesser subsequently. Once the first batch sold out, the buyers would send out an email for request for restock. Emails would usually be ignored. Messages would be sent to them via Whatsapp, which were also ignored. The last resort would be me messaging them personally, which would always get a reply.

'Oh, sorry, I missed the message from your buyer. Yes, about the restock, so sorry but we are very limited in inventory, and we have no more to give FashionValet. Once we do, we'll contact you.'

This was the standard reply from most brands, to be honest. They were telling us this but on their own platforms, they were promoting restocks. At the end of the day, it all boiled down to business. When you sell through FashionValet, you want the marketing boost for your new label. Once customers have taken notice of you, you'd naturally want to sell directly to them and cut out the middleman who took a commission (us). Why pay a middleman a portion if you can keep 100 per cent of the sales for yourself? I get it. But if every designer and brand started to feel this way, what was going to happen to FashionValet?

Designers and brands had to do what they had to do. They wanted to keep the full sales for themselves, but at the same time, they wanted to keep a good relationship with us in case they needed FashionValet at a later stage. Some would reluctantly give stock, but it came to a point where they were giving two or three pieces per design. If you didn't fall asleep in my earlier portion of this chapter, I had outlined the process of stock-handling at FashionValet. Imagine doing all of that for something that you received two pieces of. It just didn't make sense to us any more.

But what choice did we have? No stock means no revenue for us.

To address the low stock volume issue, we signed on more brands. But more brands meant heavier operations and less focus. The website grew to 500 local brands at one point, but we were losing that edge of being a *curated* place for fashion. By this time, we had to take in as many brands as possible, to the extent that there was nothing curated about us any more. It was almost as though just about anybody could join FashionValet, and I think a lot of customers could tell that we were becoming more and more like Zalora, and we were losing our way. One even called us a *'pasar malam'* (night market).

On top of that, designers close to me started expressing frustration. Some said they don't feel special any more, because FashionValet was promoting other designers whom they regarded as competitors. The nature of FashionValet has always been a place for multibrands to co-exist, but in reality, there were a lot of things I had to do to manage each designer's pride. Each had their own character, but were sensitive to their peers' work since it was such a small market to compete in. If there were any similarities between their designs and another designer/brand on FashionValet, I would receive a message asking how I could stock this other brand. If I promoted one brand more than the other, I would get questioned on why the favouritism. If I signed on Designer A whom Designer B secretly didn't like, Designer B would threaten to leave FashionValet to join Zalora. There were a lot of feelings to manage, and I tried the best I could to not stir up any drama. Some wouldn't express it to me directly, but I would always catch wind of it if brands or designers were unhappy with me or with FashionValet. I never shared any of this on my social media, and I kept my professionalism as their stockist to manage them the best I could, but it was undoubtedly hard.

It was ironic, especially because technically, some of them were not even being fair to FashionValet. They barely sent us stock, and yet they wanted explanations when we promoted someone else who *did* send us stock. The contract stated that as their stockist, FashionValet would carry all of their collections, and we stated the minimum quantity that we would need per design. Many brands breached this clause. By that time, brands had their own Instagram shops and were slowly starting to build their own websites. We found that they would launch collections that they would never send to FashionValet.

But because a lot of them have become my friends over the years, I honestly feel happy when I see their business booming. Truth be told, the fact that FashionValet helped propel them to fly high makes me smile, because at least we contributed a little to their success. I see how much passion and hard work they pour into their work, and whether they are with FV or not, I love seeing their work being rewarded and recognized. That was FV's purpose anyway; to grow the local fashion industry.

It's honestly great for them.

But it wasn't great for FashionValet.

Though I felt all sorts of happiness for them *personally*, the reality was that *professionally*, my own business was suffering. We relied on their stock to sell. If they didn't send stock, we had no sales. And we couldn't keep promoting old stock from months ago. As you probably know, fashion is fast-paced, and customers would get bored if they went to a website and kept seeing the same thing again and again. Newness is so important.

'We have so few incoming stocks in the next few months. If this goes on, there is no way we can hit our sales target,' Fadza said in a management meeting, looking very concerned about the future of the business.

'I know. I've been chasing brands for stock, but they keep saying they don't have anything new. And the ones who do give only end up giving like three pieces per design,' I explained.

'So what is the plan now?' Fadza asked me.

I felt responsible for this because brands were under me. All eyes were on me, and I could feel my face burning.

One manager broke the silence and addressed the elephant in the room. 'Since they're not following the contract, how come we are not suing them?'

With Mom, the queen of my heart, 1993

Always a Daddy's girl, 1991

Graduated with a law degree from London
School of Economics, 2009

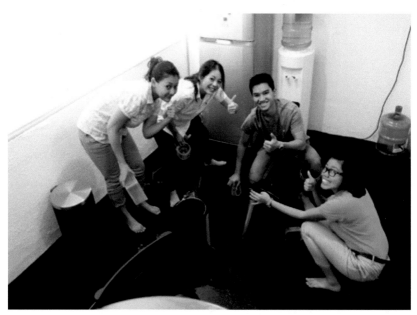

When our office flooded and ruined our red carpet, 2011

Married my partner in life and business, 2012

Our first fundraising was by taking part in a business pitching reality show where we stood in front of the nation to ask for RM 1 million investment, 2012

Signed on our first investor MyEG after winning the business pitching reality show, 2012

After a hard day's work of packing orders, 2015

Met Diane von Furstenberg in her office in New York, 2015

Young parents with our first two children Daniel and Mariam, 2015

The FashionValet team in front of our office, 2016

Shooting for *Love, Vivy* reality show about balancing mompreneurship, 2017

One of the FashionValet stores, 2017

Selected as high impact entrepreneurs in the Endeavor network, 2017

With local designers at the launch of the book *The Rise of Malaysian Designers*, written and published by FashionValet, 2017

Won Best Halal Cosmetics award for dUCk, 2018

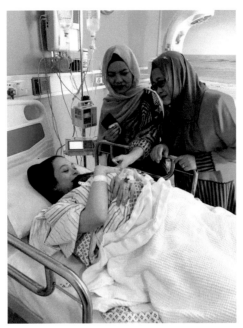

Delivered our third child Sarah with both Mom
and Mom-in-law by my side, 2018

Honoured to be one of the first local and halal brands to join Sephora, 2018

At the opening of dUCk store in KLCC mall in Kuala Lumpur, 2018

On the cover of the first-ever edition of *GLAM Hijab*, 2018

With Christine Lagarde at an event in Kuala Lumpur hosted by our Governor, 2019

Gave a talk at the LVMH office in Singapore, 2019

The original trio—Fadza, Asma' and I—celebrating FashionValet's tenth birthday, 2020

Modelling for Disney x dUCk Mulan collection which sold out in a day, 2020

With Mom and Sis at dUCk's purple library, 2021

dUCk Cafe as part of the retail experience at dUCk, 2021

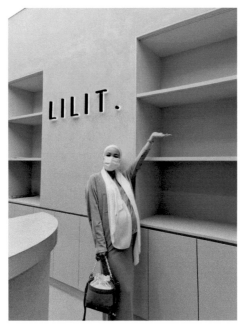

Presenting the second brand in FV Group LILIT., 2021

With retail team at dUCk store, 2022

At our warehouse, 2022

And then there were six, 2022

The four ex-tenants of my uterus, the loves of my life, 2022

Performing our *umrah* and prayers in Makkah, 2022

Chapter 6

Supporting Local Brands

'Are you crazy?' I said, laughing. 'We can't sue them, they are our bread and butter!'

The manager did not know the brands, so he was completely neutral and unbiased. To him, why sign a contract if you're not going to follow it? And if someone breached the clause, why on earth were we not taking legal action? What was a contract for, then? He was absolutely right. But I know if we started suing people in the fashion industry, we might as well say goodbye to FashionValet. We would be the hated big bad guy who was out to bully small local enterprises, which is ironic because we were actually at their mercy. Of course I'm not generalizing all of them; we had a lot of really supportive brands as well.

Fadza dismissed the idea too. 'No, no, let's not sue anybody for this. Let's look at the buying team then. Are they not liked by the brands?'

Short-term Solution

The secret to FashionValet was that the relationships were powerful. I had a connection with the brands on FashionValet, and both parties were willing to go to great lengths for each other. I respected them, and they respected me. We would have meals together, we would go to events together, we grew together so there was a bond, like I've mentioned before. But the problem with doing business this way is that it isn't scalable. Once I assigned buyers to their accounts, I no longer did the day-to-day handling of brand accounts, and that was the start of the loosening of our bond. The brands had a connection to me as a person, so a buyer coming in to handle their account was as good as having a stranger in the room. Buyers' emails and messages would be ignored and I would have to step in and message the brands personally. Only then would there be a reply. Only then would there be stocks arriving at the warehouse. It was so dependent on me that it was certainly demotivating for our buyers.

In the local fashion industry, a lot of things depend on relationships so we tried to hire buyers with good PR skills. Friendly, approachable and outgoing, so that the brands felt comfortable around them. But PR can't be all there is to a buyer because we've had buyers who became such good friends with the designers that they could not think objectively when it came to buying decisions. A good buyer must also be a person who can plan the buys and analyse the data, who is good with numbers and can monitor margins—but generally, a person like this would not be the super PR type. A person like this would be the type to email designers and say, 'From the data, your bags are doing well. We need you to send more bags by Monday. Please acknowledge email.' To which any designer would say, go fly kite. We needed to find buyers who had both skills, and this person was hard to find. It's obviously rare to find someone who was good at everything, both left and right brain.

We had some good buyers at FashionValet, but even then, the stock problem was one that could never be solved. And I realized over the years that it wasn't their fault. It's not them that was the flaw, it was the whole business model. We could not dictate what our third-party suppliers did or did not do because the stock wasn't ours. It was theirs entirely, and we only got it on consignment, so what right did we have to tell them what to do with it? Yes, we had a contract, but we could do nothing to enforce it unless we wanted to burn bridges with the entire fashion industry. On top of that, we had faults of our own, like late sales reports and payment delays as a result of our very manual processes back then.

We were not perfect either.

So I decided to try something.

Instead of waiting for their stock to arrive, which may or may not happen, we needed to be proactive instead of reactive. I decided that we should take control of our stock. Instead of carrying their existing designs, we could try doing exclusive collections instead. They design specifically for us, and we buy outright from them at a wholesale price. This way, we could request our preferences based on what our customers liked, and we could also control the quantities we got from them. Instead of their stockists, we were now their clients, who placed custom orders.

Designers and brands loved this idea too. It was a great deal for them—a bulk order with money upfront, absolutely zero risk and free marketing from us when the collection launched. Whether it sold or not, frankly, was not their problem.

From there, our exclusive collections grew, variety on the website grew and so did the excitement in the industry. Previously, we waited for the brands to decide on their own collections, which would be slower and smaller. With FashionValet creating collections with them, we funded and multiplied the activity and newness in the local fashion industry. There was an exclusive collection almost every month from designers, and this was especially heavy during Eid, which was our peak season.

On the surface, it was great for the entire ecosystem. But internally, this meant that our cash flow had to take a hit because money was flowing out in bulk, and 100 per cent of the inventory risk was on us. If the collection did not sell, it could be a potential killer for FashionValet. Our business model was a consignment model, so this was definitely a hard hit for us, but we needed to scale and being passive was not an option.

We set aside a budget to buy and tried to be as careful as we could—only buy outright designs that we knew could sell, from brands and designers that had customer demand. We loaded up on their collections throughout the year with the heaviest stocking around the Eid season, and we became the shopping hotspot for Eid outfits. The collections were beautiful, we had plenty of stock, and orders were flying out of our warehouse to customers around the world.

Now that the continuity of stock and variety problems were sorted, it was time to elevate our marketing campaigns.

Experiments in Marketing

From Day One, we had an experiment culture at FashionValet. Creativity was in the air every day at work, and we had a lot of fun trying new things that weren't common yet at that time.

In this chapter, I will share with you some of the projects that we did at FashionValet, the good ones and the bad ones.

One of our earliest marketing campaigns was for Valentine's Day, back in 2014. Whether we want to admit it or not, all men feel pressured when 14 February comes near because they know that the whole female species will be expecting something. Even if they say, 'No, it's okay, I don't want anything,' you best prepare at least a card or something to avoid getting some serious silent treatment.

'What if we reversed it?' I asked the team one day.

'What do you mean?' they asked back.

'Well, everyone expects the girl to be the recipient of Valentine's Day gift. Maybe we should challenge the status quo and ask women to get something for their men,' I suggested.

'But we only sell women's items,' the team pointed out.

'Yes, exactly. So for this week only, we can sell men's items. Shavers, playstations, games, t-shirts, ties, wallets! We can contact all the local brands that sell men's products and see if they're interested.'

'Oooh, that's cool!'

'Right? It's time we tell our women "don't be selfish, get your man something instead of just expecting to be gifted by them". In fact, our campaign should be called Don't Be Selfish!'

And the team got to work. We contacted male-focused brands, barber shops, shops that sold gadgets and games. It was so exciting because there was 100 per cent take-up rate. The male brands thought it was such a cool idea that they hadn't heard of before.

Fadza took the idea even further. He wanted the whole website to be stripped off and *only* sell these men-related products for the two days for an even bigger impact. We would be losing sales for the two days from our normal women's selection, but the buzz around this campaign might just justify that. We disabled every product on FashionValet and there was a takeover of men's products with a big 'DON'T BE SELFISH' banner on the front. We didn't expect much sales from this, but we were surprised to see that the sales matched our daily sales! No loss of income at all, *and* we had the virality.

I sent out a press release to the media, and they supported us by featuring this campaign in their publications. The word was out there, and it helped us get the buzz we needed. Men started to take notice of FashionValet from this campaign and shared it on their social media, asking their women to get something from them. They put up funny captions like, 'Finally, it's my turn!' and linked the website. The campaign got talked about from thereon, and it put us on the map with men wanting to tell their girlfriends about FashionValet's Valentine's Day campaign. 'DON'T BE SELFISH' was being shared everywhere, and it was great because it didn't cost us a single marketing dollar!

The #IAMHOMEGROWN Campaign

We also had campaigns inviting people to support local brands. This was our entire purpose, but the biggest campaign we did was the #IAMHOMEGROWN campaign in August 2017.

It was during Kuala Lumpur Fashion Week (KLFW), so the timing was perfect. That year, we sponsored KLFW, which was a big leap from where we came from, when we had to rethink even an RM 10,000 ad three times. Sponsoring the biggest fashion event in the country was a big deal for me, and it gave FashionValet an opportunity to be seen and be elevated in the local fashion industry. Again, it all boiled down to relationships. I had gotten to know Andrew, the founder of KLFW. He's been in the fashion industry much longer than us and literally knows everyone in the local fashion industry. He opened up his network to us and was very supportive for our growth.

KLFW was a three-day event. At the concourse, a grand setup was erected with a long runway and a lot of spotlights. Everyone in the mall could look on from the railings on every level, but only invited guests got to enter the area. It was exclusive, it was thrilling, it was Fashion Week. An event of that scale had many sponsors throwing themselves bidding to be a part of it, but Andrew did not want competing companies to sponsor them, so in the ecommerce category, he could only choose one ecommerce company. Whenever FashionValet offered to sponsor, he would always choose us. It made sense, he said, we both believe in the same thing—supporting the local fashion industry.

In conjunction with the event, we wanted to do a campaign to support local brands. The team wanted a cool campaign featuring several influencers who have made their names in areas of their choice. We decided to name the campaign #IAMHOMEGROWN and in the video, we would have the influencers stating their name, where they're from, their occupation and just state the phrase 'I am homegrown. Are you?' They would wear a white t-shirt with #IAMHOMEGROWN written on it in black. The vibe was edgy, the whole campaign was black and white, except for a pop of pink for the #IAMHOMEGROWN word to stand out. It was a simple concept, but it's always the simple ideas that become the best campaigns.

'Why stop at twenty? Let's feature sixty people, and make it a *huge* campaign!' I said.

We decided that we should not limit it to the fashion industry. We should feature leaders of the country, CEOs, restaurateurs, entrepreneurs, stay-at-home moms—everyone who is proud of who they are as Malaysians. I invited political activists from different parties like Dato' Seri Shahrizat Abdul Jalil and Nurul Izzah Anwar, big industry names like Aireen Omar of Air Asia and Puan Sri Tiara Jacquelina, celebrity chefs like Dato' Chef Wan, cool rappers like Joe Flizzow and Altimet, artists like Reshmonu and songwriter Najwa Mahiaddin, fashion icons like Marion Caunter and Izara Aishah, supermodels like Tuti and Tengku Azura, actors like Bront Palare and Siti Saleha, celebrity couples like actress Nora Danish and husband Nedim Nazri as well as comedian Harith Iskander and wife Dr Jezzamine Lim, and fashion photographers like Bibo Aswan and TTFGA.

All of these names came for a photo shoot in our studio. My favourite of them all was Madam Kwan from the iconic Malaysian restaurant chain Madam Kwan's. At eighty years old, she came for the photo shoot accompanied by her family, climbing up our stairs slowly but surely. I don't get starstruck at all with people, but with her, I was so nervous and in awe. I wanted so badly for her to join this campaign, and I wanted it to be as easy and as fast as possible for her. She captured the hearts of many when they saw her in the #IAMHOMEGROWN video wearing her iconic hat, because it was so unexpected.

So many cool names supported our campaign, and none of these sixty names asked for payment. I sent them a long message to introduce this campaign and each of them supported it, making the execution of the campaign so smooth for us. They loved the messaging and wanted to be a part of it, in the name of patriotism. This is an example that it's not always about who has the most money. Sometimes, it's all about being a part of something you believe in, something that has a bigger purpose.

The video was a hit. It was played before every single show at KLFW, giving us so much exposure. Life-size posters of sixty individuals were displayed inside and outside Kuala Lumpur's Pavilion Mall, including one photo of Fadza and I. I felt so proud looking at it; it felt almost unreal to me. Fadza, of course, hated it and vowed to never do photoshoots again. Outside, the event was facing the streets, where you would see a strip of these huge black-and-white posters lined up like billboards for everyone to see. There was always traffic on that road, so the number of eyeballs for this campaign was massive.

Since we were making t-shirts for the shoot, we decided to create a full-blown collection with #IAMHOMEGROWN. The FashionValet design team created a streetwear collection of t-shirts, jumpers, tunics and jogger pants with #IAMHOMEGROWN on it, and we sold it in conjunction with KLFW. We had a booth parked outside of KLFW, where we sold the items, as well as a little photoshoot area with a neon #IAMHOMEGROWN signage. Anyone could have their photo taken there, and we hired famous photographers to take these shots. The collection sold out instantly, and the whole campaign was talked about on social media. Till today, watching that #IAMHOMEGROWN video on YouTube gives me chills. I'm so proud of that campaign, which was only made possible by the team's hard work, and even prouder to find out later that a lot of marketing people used it as a case study.

In hindsight, that campaign was truly successful because of the right timing of Fashion Week, the impact of having many unexpected icons come together, and the combination of online and offline buzz. Campaigns as impactful as the #IAMHOMEGROWN one don't come often, and in today's world, where there's so much noise everywhere, it's even harder for anyone to really stand out.

The Rise of Malaysian Designers

After #IAMHOMEGROWN, we did another campaign the same year to support local designers—we wrote a book about them! It was titled *The Rise of Malaysian Designers*, and we launched it at the end of 2017.

I was inspired by coffee-table books and wanted to have one that featured twenty designers at one time. In order for people to appreciate our local fashion offerings, we first had to tell the story.

We conducted interviews with twenty designers we wanted to feature, and the final write-up was vetted by me, line by line. I remember, even near the publishing deadline, the team and I were still frantically fixing the flow of writing and checking for any grammatical mistakes. It's so nerve-racking because these books were going to print so we needed to check every word. I cannot stand printing mistakes, which has happened to us before, so you can bet that if there are any spelling mistakes in this book you're holding, I'm already curled up in bed crying over it with a big tub of ice cream going, 'Whyyyyyy?'

We had a press event for this book launch. A lot of media attended, and the room was packed with photographers. This coffee-table book was the first of its kind in Malaysia; no one had ever done a compilation of designers in one place before. We had a larger-than-life mockup of the book on stage and had every designer come up and sign it. I gave a speech and did tons of press interviews after the launch. It sure felt like the book was a success. I was already planning to have a Volume 2, because there were more designers and brands that I wanted to feature.

On the day of launch, the team and I were excited. The book had got a lot of support in the media, so it should've been good. I checked the sales.

Twenty.

What?

We only sold twenty? Twenty books sold, twenty designers featured. Was twenty a magic number here or something? How do I make it 20,000 books instead of twenty?

The sales were bad. I think we peaked at about 200 copies sold after heavy discount, and the book was soon forgotten. We realized that people liked local designers, but not enough that they would want to buy coffee-table books about them. We could also have worked with a publisher instead and had the book stocked in bookstores, instead of selling it on our own. On top of that, we received some backlash from other designers who felt hurt that they had not been featured.

A lot of lessons were learnt from this campaign. One, it taught me that customer research is important, and that was something we didn't do for this campaign. We were drinking our own kool-aid and never stopped to ask ourselves, 'How many people would actually buy a coffee-table book about local designers?' Apparently twenty.

FV Goes Offline

Marketing campaigns weren't the only things that we did. We did more physical things too, like bazaars and pop-ups.

'I've never heard of some of these brands,' was the common feedback that we got.

It made sense because local brands were not as known back then. In malls, you'd only see the international brands so you'd really have to know the local brand to be able to find them. They were on Facebook or in bazaars, and only a few would have their own physical stores in shop lots. From what we gathered, people preferred to buy international brands because they were not so confident about local brands at the time—they'd always ask us about the items' quality, sizing and price, and compare it to items from the big brands.

We figured the challenge for FashionValet was that we had to educate the customers. We didn't carry big names like ZARA, H&M, Nike or Adidas. We carried local brands that were more independent and were not mass market, so of course, people needed more time to get acquainted with them. We were essentially carrying artisan brands, and it's incredibly difficult to convince people to buy online if they haven't seen, felt or touched the items before. It was a miracle enough that we got by all these years doing that!

So we started with bazaars in the early years. It was as simple as setting up two tables below offices at first. We laid out the shoes and accessories on them, with a FashionValet website flyer to tell them about our website. We had two railings of clothes from various local brands and designers, so people could see for themselves. We sent out a newsletter: 'We'll be here on this day and this time, so please come'. Only a handful came. For all that effort standing in the hot sun for an entire day, the sales were disappointing. But hey, we had to start somewhere.

So through the years, we joined bigger bazaars. The power of collaboration was a lot stronger if more brands were involved. Word of mouth can have a much bigger reach that way, and it worked because more people came to the bigger bazaars. Our sales in bazaars increased, and it was nice to get to meet our customers face to face. We became regulars and thought maybe we could consider having a FashionValet store.

'Let's start with a pop-up first,' Fadza said, considering the commitment to opening a permanent store was no joke. We had always been an ecommerce business first, so opening stores was something new for us.

Malls at that time wouldn't entertain local brands. There was a long waiting list for international brands to enter the malls in Malaysia, so why would they even consider smaller companies? We would try and get retail contacts in the leasing departments, but we were always told nothing was available and 'we will contact you if there is'. Luckily, Fadza had a school friend working in one of the malls in Kuala Lumpur, which was Bangsar Village. In 2016, we asked him if we could open a pop-up anywhere in the mall, and after pitching to him and his bosses about FashionValet, they finally offered us a lot. It was a small lot, less than 1,000 square feet. We had hundreds of brands, so we were scratching our heads about how to furnish a store to give all brands the space they wanted. In the end, we realized we couldn't. We had to prioritize the brands that gave us the most sales—our top brands needed to have their own space in the pop-up and for the other brands, we thought we could feature them weekly on a rotational basis.

We underestimated how difficult it would be to open a store. And ours was just a pop-up! We were so used to filling up a website on screen with banners and links; not so much filling up a store with nice shelves, railings and wallpaper. We were used to emailing customers; not so much talking to them face to face. We were used to keeping a warehouse neat and tidy with clothes wrapped up nicely in plastic, but having a physical display meant we had to iron each piece of clothing and display all sizes on the store floor. Our arms were aching after ironing, making sure that there wasn't a crease visible to customers. The night before the pop-up opened to the public, I think about twenty of us came to help—some ironed, some vacuumed, some dusted, some set up the cashier, some opened boxes, some cleared empty boxes, some got us all dinner. Exhausting would be an understatement, but we kept going because we were so proud that now there was a place for local brands to be showcased to the public—in a legit mall!

The pop-up was only for three months but did so well in terms of sales. We covered the rent early on, and even we were shocked at how well it did.

'It looks so different in real life,' customers would tell us. And when they were in the store, the tendency to convert a look into a purchase was higher. We could tell the customers about the various brands with passion and excitement in our eyes. Customers would also browse longer in-store and end up buying more than just the item that they had originally planned to buy.

At the end of the pop-up, the mall offered us a permanent location. Fadza and I looked at each other, hesitant at first. We were not planning to open stores, but we knew that because we were carrying local brands that were lesser-known, we needed to have a physical presence so customers could discover them. Only then could the customers fall in love with local brands. How could we expect customers to love a brand they could only see on screen?

Thus began the start of a series of FashionValet stores. Brands felt so proud of this that they too came to check out the stores, and some even fixed the displays to make them even better. It was a matter of collective pride for the local fashion industry. Among the big brands you see in malls, you could now see FashionValet stores too—the house of local brands.

The Reality Show

The biggest experiment that we did was probably the reality show *Love, Vivy*. The idea I had was completely different from the outcome, and I'll share with you the story.

The competition was tough, circa 2016. More and more websites came up, social media was lowering the barriers of entry, and everyone was marketing something, so it got harder and harder to stay ahead.

The two biggest fashion websites were still Zalora and FashionValet, but Zalora was carrying all sorts of international brands like Nike, Adidas and Topshop, so we had come to regard them less and less as a competitor. They were clearly a giant marketplace that sold everything fashion, whereas FashionValet was a niche player focusing on local fashion only, and the distinction was becoming clearer and clearer to the public.

Zalora wasn't the problem any more. It was the sudden emergence of individuals wanting to do local fashion hubs like ours, after seeing the 'success' of FashionValet. I never underestimated anyone, and I never rested. I knew that any one of them could overtake FashionValet if we didn't constantly innovate with new ideas.

At that time, ecommerce was rising—it had a certain glamour attached to it, and people thought it was a sexy industry. On my social media, I would post about my working life and people always wanted to know how it feels working in an ecommerce company. So I thought, why not open our doors and literally show them? I was inspired by the show on E!, *House of DVF*, where Diane Von Furstenberg let us into her work life, and we got to see her office, her team and their challenges. I found it so exciting and wondered if we could do the same. What about a reality show showing the ins and outs of our jobs—the good stuff, the bad stuff, no holds barred? Every website crash, every bad deal made, I wanted to share it with the world. Number one, it would be great marketing for FashionValet. Number two, it could inspire other entrepreneurs to chase their own dreams.

I was lucky enough to meet Diane Von Furstenberg in person in New York in 2015. I was part of a fashion tour organized by Endeavor Global (a global network of entrepreneurs) and FashionValet was the only company selected from Malaysia to come. Fadza and I flew to New York and met all sorts of cool companies like Google, Tory Burch, Melissa Shoes and DVF herself. I still have the photo of her kissing my cheek and telling me she thought I was cute (it pays to be short, everyone instantly likes you because you're 'cute'). At the session with DVF, I asked her if there was any advice she could give me if I wanted to make my own reality show about my company. She looked at me and said, 'Make sure you control the narrative.' A piece of advice that I wish I had taken more seriously.

I came back home to Malaysia and started planning this reality show. I kept it top-secret because I didn't want people to know yet.

The industry is so small that if word got around, my competitors could take this idea and launch theirs first. Again, my competitive side needed me to be the first to do this.

The team and I had a meeting with the leads in Astro, and we discussed this idea—the first reality show about an ecommerce company in Malaysia and the juicy behind-the-scenes of running it. We had plenty of drama as well as lessons to share that would benefit others running their own companies. By this time, FashionValet was already an established name, so I had no doubt that this could work.

Astro got back to me with their thoughts. Number one, if we wanted to feature FashionValet as a company, it would be considered branded content, so we would have to pay massive amounts of money because every episode was considered an advertisement spot. It was just like paying for the thirty-second commercial slots, except you're paying even more. This time it wasn't thirty-second; it was a thirty-*minute* slot for each episode!

Number 2, they had another proposal. They said that the angle of the show should be centred around *me* as the personality. Make it a Vivy Yusof reality show so that we could cover a balance between work and personal life. This way, it doesn't have to be about ecommerce per se, but about juggling entrepreneurship and life altogether. Make it an even bigger purpose to inspire budding entrepreneurs out there, especially women entrepreneurs. They also shared that business-related content doesn't get as much of a response—the reality of TV was that people wanted to see *personalities,* not businesses.

Fadza was uncomfortable with this and made it known from the start, but I pushed on. I was already sharing my personal life on social media so this wasn't anything new for me (boy, did I underestimate TV reach . . .). We were also in a unique position because FashionValet already had a public face (me), and we had always started this way, since my blogging days. I was a walking billboard for the company, so why not milk my brand while we were still on top?

Deferring to the experts in content and its ratings, we took Astro's advice. I can't reveal the financial terms of the partnership, but it was an offer we could not refuse. On top of that, I still got to have a say on how every single episode was to be done. I insisted that every episode must be heavier on the business angle than the personal life angle, and Astro agreed to it. We also agreed to launch this during the Ramadhan period to fully maximize the reach during our peak shopping season, Eid.

They needed my name in the title of the show. So I suggested *Sincerely, Vivy*. Since I love writing, and my whole career started from my blog, I thought it would be nice to have it as a sign-off. Every episode ended with a narration by me about the lessons I learnt, and I would end it with 'Sincerely, Vivy'. I loved it. Astro didn't. Their feedback was that the word 'sincerely' was too long and not very friendly to the mass TV consumers. They suggested *Love, Vivy* and we went with that, even though I cringed at first.

Since this was a show that depicted us, I didn't want to compromise on quality. The content had to be good, the cinematography had to be professional, the camera quality had to be top-notch. I worked again with the amazing couple Fauzi and Nazura from CelebrateTV (remember them from Chapter 4?), who were already like family to me. Together with me, they became the co-producers for the *Love, Vivy* reality show that we aired on Astro Ria.

The CelebrateTV team poured their hearts into the *Love, Vivy* project, directed by a talented man named Faiz. There was a huge board in their office that had all the episodes broken down. Post-it notes were everywhere on it, colour-coded. Blue was work-life content, and pink was personal-life content. I made it clear that I needed more blues on the board so we added a feature for one local designer in every episode.

We began the shooting of *Love, Vivy*, and I really underestimated the work needed for it. The shoots ran from early morning until late at night, almost every single day. Every scene had to wait for extensive lighting setup, and after every scene, we had to set up for the interview part of the show. Multiple people had to be interviewed; the team, my family, Fadza and myself. A lot of the scenes were in multiple places, so we had to mobilize everyone from the cast to the production team to any external people we had in that episode. Whenever we shot outside, we had to ask for permission to shoot, and when we couldn't get it, the whole episode had to be tweaked. It was especially tough when we had to shoot overseas, like in London, Singapore and Brunei. *Love, Vivy* was a lot of work, and it ate into my *actual* work in the office. It was then that I developed so much respect for the Kardashians. Man, twenty seasons of this? Mad respect.

My work in the office piled up, and I found myself sleeping two or three hours a night because I would spend late nights catching up on work. Fadza and I barely got any time together because we hardly saw each other during the day, so we ended up arguing a lot. On top of that, we were parents of two now, with the arrival of our beautiful daughter, Mariam. I was still adjusting to being a working mom of two kids and having the constant guilt that I wasn't doing enough—for Mariam, especially. It was crazy, and I remember Fadza tearing up after we wrapped the season because (a) he was proud of me but also (b) he could have his wife back. He saw firsthand how I was like a walking zombie towards the end of it all. Even I don't know how I pulled it off, not having any experience in this showbiz thingy, but it was an experience I will always cherish.

Season 1 aired in April 2016 and was very well-received. We saw a rise in traffic every week when our episode aired and a rise in our social media following, too. I got messages every day throughout the season from followers and strangers saying that they loved the show. And this was without any other marketing boost like digital ads or billboards or anything. It was purely on the channel and social media accounts.

A year later, we discussed the possibility of Season 2. During the discussion, Astro pulled up all the data from Season 1 to show us what people liked and what people didn't like so that we could improve for this season. The data showed that people stayed on during the personal life parts, and they changed the channel when it was a work part, where I interacted with local designers. Basically, the content with local designers did not work for TV, and the content with family, instead, saw a surge of interest. People wanted to know more about my family life or drama at work. At least, that was what the data said. *Love, Vivy* was also the first show of its kind to show the balance between professional and personal life, so we could not do any apple to apple comparison with any similar shows on Astro.

Seeing how well Season 1 did for the business, we decided to keep the momentum going with a Season 2 that had even more episodes; thirteen, almost double that of Season 1. We took Astro's advice and threw in way more personal-life content. There were family holidays, there were more sessions with my mom and mom-in-law, there was a lot more of the kids. It was more entertaining and that one episode of mom buying *apam balik* by the roadside was such a hit that even my mom became famous. She couldn't go anywhere in public without someone recognizing her and wanting a photo.

My kids were on another level. At that time, it was just Daniel and Mariam. People took photos of them in malls, people kissed their cheeks at public events, there was even a time when I was eating with the kids at a food court and a lady came to sit with us and started talking to Daniel and Mariam. Fadza grew extremely uncomfortable with all the eyes on us when we walked in public and people stopping me for photos every day. Even when we had our romantic meals, people would take photos of me eating or come up to our table for a photo. At first, it was flattering, but after a while, it did not feel normal any more. Our kids were being watched, and we grew paranoid. It was different if we wanted the celebrity life, but the truth was that we were not cut out for that—we were just entrepreneurs who needed to grow our business.

We faced a dilemma: *Love, Vivy* had reached 6.3 million viewers on TV and that was doing great things for the business, but our paranoia grew as our privacy declined. The business was growing, but at the expense of my personal life. My life was exposed to a reach so big beyond my own following that, just as the supporters grew, I also invited the attention of another group—the haters. They found anything they could to hate me—I was seen as 'too modern', 'too bossy', 'spoke English too much', and many other 'too's. I guess that's the price of showbiz—you get your fair share of lovers but also haters.

I got caught up in the glam of it all. In the race to increase our ratings, I had lost the narrative of what this show was supposed to be about—the business. I had become obsessed with what worked for ratings, and I lost myself in the process. I had a lot of fun filming it and felt very proud when I saw FashionValet on TV, but people started regarding me as a celebrity and featuring me on gossip sites. As an entrepreneur, I felt like a little bit of my credibility was lost among the entrepreneurs as I was seen more as a 'celebrity entrepreneur'. I hate that phrase.

This was when DVF's advice played in my head. *Make sure you control the narrative.*

I was buying bubble tea one day, when the lady who took my order said, 'Oh my god, you're that actress that plays a businesswoman character!'

What?

No no, I *am* the businesswoman. I'm not acting as one.

I *am* one.

Oh, no.

I think I lost the narrative, Diane.

Chapter 7

Starting House Brands

That was not the only narrative I lost control of.

The Problem with Buying Outright

Because we were buying outright from designers and brands, they now knew we were willing and able to pay upfront. Suddenly, a lot of brands requested for outright purchase of their stock as opposed to the consignment model. If we said no, some of these brands would say they would go to Zalora instead or slowly stop sending stock to us. My solution to the stock problem had dug a bigger hole for us—now everyone wanted an outright buy.

If you ask any budding local designers out there, most might say that the biggest challenge is the funds or capital to make new collections. If there are no investors or fund injections involved, they have to wait for the proceeds from the previous collection sales to roll over to produce the next collection, which may take months. Understandably, the consignment model won't be the preferred model for smaller brands because they have to reduce their small margin to even smaller margin *and* wait for long payment terms by platforms like us. Outright buys are the best deals for them—money upfront, with absolutely zero risk. The risk was passed to us 100 per cent. Whether or not the collection did well would not affect them financially.

The truth remained that we desperately needed products; we desperately needed supplies from our vendors. No new products coming into the warehouse meant no new revenue for us. We considered dropship as a model—a marketplace where products were shipped out directly from designers and brands to the customers. We tested it out with a few brands, but customer frustration grew because deliveries were either sent at different times or were delayed or were not in good condition. In some cases, they weren't delivered at all because the brand had forgotten to ship them out. Customers grew frustrated with the inconsistencies of service, so we decided to scrap the model. We needed to control the service level—that was a non-negotiable after this episode.

So outright buying it was. We agreed to buy outright the collections from brands that had good historical data. We even took some risks to try out new brands by buying a small collection first to test the waters. For some, we financed the entire production and did a profit split. There were different models that we tried, depending on how confident we were in the collection.

Problems started arising. First of all, there were ridiculous MOQs to fulfil (minimum order quantity, or the minimum number of pieces that you had to buy)—one collection could have 3,000 to 5,000 pieces of clothes that we were obligated to buy as a minimum. Designers and brands didn't have a choice because this was the MOQ that their suppliers had set (most suppliers in China won't entertain you if you order in small quantities). I understood but it also made me really uncomfortable because I knew I couldn't sell that much from *one* brand. Even when I checked past data, their sales on FashionValet were nowhere near this figure. So how could I justify such an order? Do I just do it so I don't lose them?

Secondly, the prices are set by the designers and brands. Some pieces had prices that didn't make sense—a plain top for RM 600?

A plain dress for RM 1,500? We weren't a luxury platform. And we had to buy MOQ, which meant we had to sell hundreds, sometimes thousands of pieces of these. It was the designers and brands' prerogative to set their own collection's prices, of course, and they knew their own quality well, so I wouldn't ever dispute their prices. They needed to make money too. But it certainly was not an easy challenge to sell these kinds of prices at these kinds of quantities from brands that were not yet globally known. Of course, we thought the world of them, but the reality remained that we carried local brands that not everyone knew about. The choice was ours now: do we buy this collection and take all the risk, or do we risk losing them? Because if we didn't buy it, 'Zalora has called to enquire' would come up a lot.

This constant dilemma was my life for several years as an entrepreneur. I felt like I was between a rock and a hard place, with no choice but to adhere to *any* requests because if I didn't, we'd have no stock, i.e., no sales. I can't tell you enough what a crappy position this was to be in, knowing that my company's rice bowl was dependent on third parties that I had no control over. On the one hand, if I didn't buy outright and just stuck to the consignment model, we would have to beg for stock that was limited in supply to begin with. On the other hand, if we bought collections outright from designers and brands with these kinds of MOQ and fixed prices, we would be left with so much dead inventory that it would kill us. Either way, FashionValet was screwed.

Stress level 300. Out of 10.

The feeling of not being in control of your own supply, and ultimately your own business, kept me up at night a lot. Here we were, financing and growing *other* people's businesses and footing all of the risks. It was so much simpler and fulfilling in the beginning when FashionValet had just started. How did it change so drastically? I grew frustrated and I grew worried.

I hope what you can pick up from my first decade is this: you have to control as much as you can in your own company. Try to avoid being in a position where your fate rests on someone else's yes or no.

Hello, Wholesale

Finally, we decided that we had to take control of our own supply. It wasn't part of the plan, but it was a survival response. We needed more variety on the website, and we were desperate for more stock, which the local brands could not give us. Whenever something sold out, we couldn't get restock from them so it was frustrating, to say the least. We needed sales to help us grow, or rather, survive, so we had to figure out how to get stock independently, which we could control.

Circa 2013, we found out about wholesale malls in Bangkok, so we made a trip there to check them out. We found so many things that we knew our customers would love, and bought them. The mall was huge and bustling, but we still bumped into Malaysian brands and boutiques that also bought from these wholesalers. That's why you see some brands selling the exact same things sometimes—because they bought it from the same supplier, or their suppliers bought from the same source manufacturer. It's a whole chain in the ecosystem. A lot of the times in this mall, people avoided eye contact with one another because they don't want you to know where they bought their inventory.

But the wholesale business was very interesting to me. You only get a couple of days in this huge place, and you have to buy as much inventory as possible. You get B-U-S-Y and there is no time for chitchat or Instagram. It is go, go, go. So we'd split and move to different areas of the mall to cover more. Divide and conquer! It was an adrenaline rush all day long, followed by lots of snoring at night because everyone would be so tired.

A lot of negotiations and haggling could be seen here, and I watched others do it as much as I did it myself. It was like a game, so thrilling and so fun to see who would win. Sometimes, the trick is to walk away, and the supplier will call you back to match your offer price. Sometimes, the trick is to say you'll come back with even more business so the supplier would agree in hopes of future orders. Sometimes, the trick is to pretend you can't speak the same language so the supplier gets so frustrated they just agree to stop the agony of communicating

with you. If you have time, visit a wholesale mall one of these days—
you'll learn a lot about human beings just by people-watching.

We lugged around huge trolley bags to stuff our purchases in,
which we then transferred to our suitcases. At the time, we only bought
ten or twenty pieces per design, so it was manageable. As the business
grew, we had to buy more and have funny memories of each other
sitting and jumping on suitcases to squish everything together. 'WHY
WON'T YOU FIT?!' we would wail at the suitcases, as if it was the
suitcases' fault.

We also learnt a lot about our customers—what colours they liked,
what silhouettes they liked—and we based our buying decisions on that.
As opposed to the consignment model, where we had no choice but to
just take in whatever the designers and brands sent to us. Whether or
not the customers liked it, that was all we had. If something sold out,
we couldn't restock it if the brand had run out. Discovering wholesale
was like discovering a gold mine! For the first time, we could control
the incoming supply and even curate them to suit our customers, both
the quantity *and* price.

After Bangkok, we tested out other wholesale spots in Indonesia
and a couple of other places. We found that Bangkok had a lot of
trendy pieces, and Indonesia had more modest fashion pieces, so
to put everything under the one brand didn't make sense. So we
decided to create more brands that would house the different kinds
of fashion styles. One brand would carry the more trendy pieces
from Bangkok, and another brand would carry the modest fashion
pieces from Indonesia.

And that was the beginning of the new FashionValet—a platform
of local brands and a couple of house brands, too. It now extended
to more than just local brands, which wasn't the original plan, but we
were forced to think of creative ways to get stock that our customers
would love.

It worked because we started seeing revenues grow from house
brands and, best of all, margins improved. The moment we could
control our supply, everything seemed so simple to scale. If we needed to
restock, we would just order more and they would come in a few days.

We were able to keep the momentum going for bestsellers and really maximize the sales from them.

But soon after, we met with a problem.

A brand was dropping off stock, and we were doing the QC for the items. When I held one of the designs up, I recalled seeing the exact same one that we had bought from Bangkok. It was a pink floral top.

'Oh my god, guys, we have the same product as this brand,' I alerted the team.

We can't have two of the same design launching on the website!

Worse, they were priced differently.

The brand would be so upset if we sold the same floral top. So we held ours back and launched the brand's ones first. Once those sold out, only then did we launch ours. Priority has to be given to our vendor, I had thought then.

This happened more often, and it really disrupted our operations. We had to check one by one that the designs we bought wholesale didn't overlap with designs from the brands we carried. In fact, there were many instances when one brand's designs were the same, or similar, to another brand's designs. These overlaps happened often, and we tried our best to control things by launching one first and holding back the other. But it became impossible after a while because it was all very manual. We not only had to check overlaps between brands, but also overlaps between those brands and our own wholesale stock.

We decided to stop the wholesale method because it was causing too many overlaps with the brands we carried. And so it disappeared, the wholesale model that we experimented with. It was short-lived and was good while it lasted. I'm glad we tried it out because it forced us to go a step further, a step I didn't know would help the company indefinitely.

FashionValet then entered into an unknown world—*producing* our own clothes.

Building Brands from Scratch

This was unknown to us because prior to this, we were just the middleman—we sourced from other people, and we sold to our customers. Now, we were getting involved with manufacturing as well. Would that be the right move? Should we be getting into this new business we knew nothing about?

But what choice did we have? It's either this or keep on begging and hoping for stock (and sales) that may or may not come.

Looking back now, after a decade, this was the best decision we made as a company, and we wouldn't be where we are today if we hadn't jumped into it. It's crazy how you end up at a place you never planned to be in. Creating our own brands and producing our own clothes was never written in our business plan. We were going to be a platform for local brands—that's it!

I remembered a quote from Marc Randolph's *Netflix* book when he talked about business plans, 'Go ahead and write up a plan but don't put too much faith into it.' I finally understood that. Life throws you at crossroads and shows you all sorts of signs. When you feel at your lowest and you feel lost, look from another angle and you'll see that all those challenges had been signs all along to pivot. Be comfortable with change.

If you follow your business plan too rigidly and fail to adapt, you die.

The Start of Our In-house Brands

We had a platform that had a lot of traffic, we had loyal customers who loved fashion, and we discovered that we had a knack for growing brands. For all these years, I'm giving feedback to other people's brands. I'm giving other people ideas on collections and marketing campaigns that they might not even want. I have so much excitement for creative campaigns and beautiful collections, but no one specific outlet to pour it all into. All the brands I communicate with aren't mine to grow fully, so the satisfaction is not quite the same. So why not create our own brands? Fadza and I asked each other. Not the wholesale kind of brands, but brands made from scratch. Ones that we build from the ground up in all areas, from design to manufacturing to marketing to branding to retail to managing their own profits and losses (P&Ls).

And that was the start of the new era of FashionValet. We created several brands over the decade, the first one being FV Basics—a line selling only basic wear to complement the third-party items on FashionValet. In May 2014, we created dUCk, a premium modest fashion brand that we started with just a line of scarves.

We were already used to hunting for designers and brands, but now we had to add another kind of hunt—clothing manufacturers.

Everyone told me China was *the* place for manufacturers. So I checked it out. It was a challenge because I had never been there before and language was going to be a challenge. 'Ni *hao ma*' alone was not exactly going to help me survive. When we started our own house brands, we used agents for a while because we were not familiar with the manufacturing industry or China, really. The agents would fly back and forth between Kuala Lumpur and China, to help with our production—they were the middlemen between us and the Chinese manufacturers. The clothes and scarves would arrive at ours, even when we had never met the manufacturer or seen the factory. But I was longing to see things for myself. I found it bizarre that I didn't know this industry when I was literally *investing* in it.

With a Chinese friend of ours, Fadza and I went to China for the first time in 2016 to see the entire manufacturing landscape. Thank God for Chinese colleagues because that's the only reason we survived there. The language barrier is a huge problem there, and it was very intimidating to do business in China at first. Even today, I struggle whenever I make trips there and despite all the translation apps, I can't even get a Starbucks order right. 'Frappucino, cream-based, without whipped cream' translated on the app would get an eye squint from the barista, who would then discuss with other baristas, who would then scratch their heads, and in the end, I would get a hot caramel macchiato. Either the app translated wrong or they thought I was being difficult. Maybe both.

My experience going there was overwhelming. Back then, you had to know people to help you move around. It wasn't like now, when everything is digital and the language barrier can be easily figured out.

During that first trip there, we went to visit our existing manufacturers, but also some potential new ones. We were taken to see a few manufacturers—from proper big buildings to dodgy rooms in alleys. One place we went to was almost entirely dark; it was on the third floor and locked from the *outside*, and when we went in, there were a couple of men sewing, who avoided eye contact with us at all times. There were trays of food and dirty plates in one corner, so I'm guessing they had their meals in there. There were fabric piles everywhere on the floor, and I could've sworn I saw something moving—maybe rats! I wanted to leave immediately because I was so scared, and I couldn't help but wonder if the clothes I bought in shops were being made in those kinds of conditions. Why was the door locked? I was told not to ask any questions, so out of fear, I restrained myself. *Always visit your suppliers' factories,* I made a mental note.

We also visited the fabric market in China, where I transformed into a little kid in Disneyland. It was unimaginably huge, with endless mini shops of fabric swatches and rolls. I jumped for joy when I saw beautiful prints and beautiful lace that I could imagine being turned into a gorgeous collection. I'm no designer, but I liked fashion enough to be able to appreciate a place like that.

That visit opened up our eyes to a whole other world that was possible for us. I realized we knew so little prior to it. Seeing the possibilities out there, I really wanted to go all out to grow our house brands.

Besides FV Basics, dUCk is an example of a brand created by us that swept the market. Whenever dUCk launched new collections, the website could not take the load of traffic and would often crash. When we opened stores, there would be queues outside the FashionValet stores as early as 5.30 a.m., of customers who wanted to buy the collections. When dUCk joined bazaars, other vendors would complain because our queues would block their booths. dUCk items were selling out within minutes after they launched, and customers got so anxious that even our store teams were asked to take off their scarves so customers could buy them. People would even resell dUCk in a secondary market, and people started labelling dUCk as the 'Supreme' of modest fashion. It was exciting and phenomenal! More on dUCk in the next chapter.

We also continued a brand we called Aleena, which focused on modest fashion apparel. Modest fashion is a huge industry that offers apparel catered to the Muslim market, and it seemed to be what our customers responded to the most, so that was what we did more of. Being where we are now as a modest fashion group was definitely thanks to our customers nudging us in that direction.

We saw what this move of having our own house brands did to our business—it just *boomed*. Margins were so much better because we controlled cost and pricing, and sales were so much better because we could control the designs.

Best of all, we had a lot of fun building our own brands and seemed to be really good at it. Seeing the growth of all our house brands made us crave for more. Perhaps due to the pressure of wanting to grow the group so big so fast, we decided to go all out for building brands. A little bit too gung-ho, but good luck trying to tell an entrepreneur to slow down . . .

I reached out to people I admired when it came to fashion—people who were different, people who had creative minds and could make ideas come to life. Till today, I feel like I can spot these individuals whenever I come across them—it's not just about them looking fashionable at Fashion Week, it's about having that grit and passion to want to build long-lasting standout brands with substance.

I reached out to fashion blogger Raja Nadia Sabrina, and we created a brand called 'aere' together. The brand was very much a reflection of her style—feminine, flowy, dreamy. We gave her creative freedom on how she wanted to run aere, from design to marketing, while we financed the entire operations of the brand from team salaries to rentals to production to marketing. We really invested into aere to propel its growth, making multiple collections a year, hosting marketing events and even joining fashion weeks in KL, Jakarta and Dubai. Sabrina and aere were featured in multiple publications, and I was so proud to see their growth.

Aere quickly became one of FashionValet's top brands by sales, which shows how well the brand was doing. In fashion, a lot of it is glitz and glam, but there is no point if the numbers at the end of the day are nowhere near the glitz and glam. Aere had both—which was also due to Sabrina's understanding of both the creative side and the commercial side of running a business. She knew what aere customers wanted, she knew what would sell and what would not, and a creative director like her was a rare find. She was a gem.

The promising traction from FV Basics, dUCk, Aleena and aere gave me the confidence that we indeed knew our stuff when it came to building brands, so I went on a spree to build more brands. I found other gems in the industry for us to build brands with—two of them being Indonesian fashion blogger Diana Rikasari and Malaysian fashion icon Tengku Chanela Jamidah.

With Diana, we created SchmileyMo from scratch—a happy-go-lucky brand that creates fun and quirky collections, much like Diana herself. Jamidah had an existing brand that we acquired, Thavia—a brand that exuded a cool factor and had a kind of branding that I knew could go international pretty easily. I was excited about both brands, and again, like aere, we gave both creative directors freedom in creating their collections. Diana wanted to create a collection out of colourful breakfast bowls; we said go ahead. Jamidah wanted to shoot with bald female models in the desert; we cheered her on. It was so interesting to watch creative concepts unfold right before our eyes, and each brand was so different that I was surrounded by creativity left, right and centre. Just like aere, we financed the entire production and operations of running SchmileyMo and Thavia too, and put them in Fashion Weeks and the media. Both brands bloomed, and SchmileyMo was even in talks to be stocked on the popular UK website www.asos.com.

All these brands under our group brought variety and life to the website, and it was truly an exciting time at FashionValet.

In the excitement of it all, I think I went too far with my ambition of wanting to build too many brands too fast. Even though the brands we created were all distinct from one another, our focus was inevitably split. Soon, we became jack of all trades and master of none. Resources had to be split among all these brands, with resentment brewing if more resources went to one brand than the other. Even if I thought they were justified by sales and growth, it was always a tough conversation to have.

There was also the challenge of working with creative directors whose personas are tied to the brand. For example, Raja Nadia Sabrina fell sick, unfortunately, and even though she wanted to push on, it took a toll on her deteriorating health at the time. We were at a point when we had to discuss the future of aere, and we decided to hand the ownership of the brand back to her, so she could one day grow it back on her own terms. Another example was Thavia, where Tengku Chanela Jamidah moved to the States because of family reasons. We tried to carry on with virtual meetings, but it was always tough because of the time difference and the entire nature of fashion, which requires you to touch and feel the fabrics and samples.

With all these factors, I'm always cautious now to start brands that are tied to a person. I loved working with each of them and witnessing such creativities and unique qualities of others, but it was too risky for the entire business.

But I didn't know all this back then.

At that time, it finally felt like we had put an end to the stock problem that we previously had. Now the website was bustling with variety, thanks to the three different business models that we had:

1. Third-party brands (consignment and outright purchase)
2. FashionValet's own collaborations with celebrities and designers, and
3. Our own group of house brands.

Surely we were ready to go overseas, right?

But to understand the 'going international' episode better, I have to tell you all about this one purple brand, dUCk.

Chapter 8

A dUCk Is Born

'When are you going to wear the hijab?' my mom would ask a lot.

'Soon, Ma,' I'd tell her.

hides all photos of me in miniskirts in a locked drawer

A typical girl growing up, I was always interested in dressing up. My hair was always nicely blown, with brown highlights. I would always experiment with my fashion style—miniskirts, sleeveless, tube dresses, I've done them all. I'd post outfit photos on the blog, and it would garner more engagement from people. Brands started reaching out to sponsor me, wanting me to promote their items to my readers. I was on a high.

I remember my mom freaking out one time when she saw photos of my outfit on my blog. 'Astarghfirullah!' she exclaimed. My dad was a lot cooler. *googles *how to block your mother from your blog**

I loved fashion, I loved dressing up, I loved my nice hair.

Growing up, wearing a hijab was the last thing on my mind.

My mom would nag about it all the time, so my rebellious hormones were like 'na-ah no thanks'. We'd mostly see our moms and older women wearing the hijab, so there was no young role model hijabi

I could aspire to be like, or at least none that I knew of. My friends didn't wear the hijab and judging from our clubbing photos, I don't think hijab was on *their* to-do list either.

I told my mom I'd cover up after I graduated, just to soothe her. Graduation, engagement, wedding . . . still no hijab.

It's true when they say God will open your heart whenever He feels like it.

Out of nowhere, after birthing my first son, Daniel, I had the urge.

Maybe it was the sense of wanting to grow up. Maybe it was a sense of responsibility. Maybe it was a deeper understanding of religion. I wasn't the most devout, but I had been joining religious talks here and there with my friends—and I enjoyed it. It was different from the old-school Ustaz telling you to do things this way or else. I could never relate to those Islamic classes as a child. Everything was 'do this do that, here are the rules, don't question'. 'Memorize this, pray five times a day, don't eat or drink during Ramadhan' is what we're told, but there are stories and values behind all of these. My parents would always try to teach me the stories and values, but when your heart isn't ready to listen, all you hear are words. Faith really is a journey, unique to the individual—it cannot be forced. Everyone has their own spiritual journey with different timelines and milestones.

I soon learnt that the hijab is not just confined to a piece of scarf—it is a wholesome 360-degree representation of a Muslim's lifestyle. The way we dress, the way we speak, the way we walk, the way we respect others, all this is hijab too. I understood deeper and wanted to learn more, on my own. Suddenly, I felt proud to be Muslim; suddenly, I felt closer to God and wanted to be *seen* as a Muslim. I started praying more, I started appreciating the time on the prayer mat as a time to reflect and connect with the Creator, and most importantly, I started feeling gratitude. Here I had a life full of colour—great parents, great husband, a growing business, and on top of all that, God granted me a child, too. I had a roof over my head, food on the table and an able body to work with. What had I done to show my gratitude to Him?

Just like that, I thought to myself, *Wow, I want to wear the hijab. For Him.*

I didn't waste any time. #asusual #impatientme

I told Fadza and immediately bought a bunch of scarves. That night, I wore one out to dinner, feeling conscious but excited. Somehow, though, I felt even more beautiful and polished in it. I felt elegant.

The next day, I wore it to work and announced it on my Instagram. People were shocked. I mean, the outfit post before that was me in a tight tank top showing cleavage.

Though I felt good, I was a little worried about the business. I was the face of FashionValet. Now, I could no longer promote and wear the brands selling non-modest fashion items on our platform. I also didn't know how I would be perceived in the fashion industry. In 2013, hijab in the young and hip fashion industry wasn't as big as it is now. At that time, I was gracing fashion magazines and newspapers. Did this new look have a place there? That question was answered when a renowned fashion magazine cancelled a shoot with me after I wore the hijab, saying, 'We decided to go in a different direction'. *Oh no, I was going to be ousted from the fashion industry*, I thought as I worried about FashionValet.

But Islam really is the gift that keeps on giving. Soon after, so many doors opened for me. My followers on social media increased, my blog readership went up, and I was getting messages telling me that they were so glad they now had a young hijab icon to follow. Over the months, I got messages that people started wearing the hijab after seeing me wear it and thanked me for making it look easy. If only they knew the years of nagging from my mother and the countless tries of me wrapping my scarf in front of the mirror and failing.

The business grew, too. The scarves category saw such traction that we couldn't keep up with getting stocks in. Brands started sending us stock with more modest designs like long sleeves, and even started their own lines of headscarves. Magazines started calling again, and I'm proud to say the magazine that cancelled on me, not only eventually did an interview with me but also put me on their cover. Who says modest fashion can't be front and centre?

It was extraordinary what I was experiencing. I realized then that the hijab topic was probably on every young Muslim girl's mind. They probably had their own moms nagging at them, too.

They probably worried if the hijab might change their lifestyles, too. They probably wondered if they had to change their entire wardrobe, too. They were probably curious about the hijab too, but felt worried to embrace it and go all in.

They just needed someone they could relate to . . . and moms don't count.

There's Gotta Be a Better Way

The wardrobe thing is a valid concern, though. With a headscarf came so many expectations. I shopped for the scarves first, so I still wore my normal clothes, some of them tight or short. I'd get comments on Instagram telling me to wear hijab 'properly' and that if I didn't know how to wear it, 'then just take it off'. Some people made the experience very unwelcoming and, frankly, intimidating. I honestly think this is one of the reasons people take the hijab off, because they're constantly being judged and nothing will be good enough for the online audience.

'I can see your neck, I can see your ankles, I can see your arm.'

Okay. But can you see my personality, my efforts and my love for others?

People can make the journey harder, but you must keep your eyes on the prize. Take your time but be sincere about your intentions to Him. In God's eyes, you're probably someone who is so loved by Him because you're constantly trying to be a better person.

And constantly try was exactly what I did.

Getting used to the scarf took time, and shopping for it was overwhelming, to say the least.

Here I was thinking, okay cool I'm going to buy a couple of new headscarves today.

Nope.

'Here is the jersey material and chiffon material and silk material, which one are you looking for? Here are all the inners, do you want the no-neck one or the ones with neck or the magic inners? And here are all the pins, do you want the safety pin or the normal ones or magnetic pins? Oh, what about brooches and chin pins? We have a whole section for you to choose from. Ah, do you need the volumizer, too?'

WHAT?

Hold on, I'm still on magic inner.

What the fruit is a magic inner?

(Fun fact: This exact experience is what led me to make The Starter Kit at dUCk. One box with all the essentials that you need when you want to start wearing the hijab, complete with a message from a friend telling you that you got this.)

Over the next few months, I collected all sorts of scarves, accessories and inners, magic and not-so-magic. I was excited about my journey, but somehow, the shopping experience didn't mirror my excitement. I'd go from shop to shop, and they would sell me the scarf like it was just another thing. I didn't feel like it was a celebration, I didn't feel special at all. Every scarf was just folded into a plastic bag, and you just paid and moved on with your life. There was nothing aspirational or special about the experience.

There's gotta be a better way, one that makes women feel celebrated when they hit this personal milestone.

'There's gotta be a better way'—the start of every business idea.

I contrasted that with brands that *did* make me feel special— Hermes, LV, Dior. Sure, these are luxury brands but we can still extract the way they make anyone *feel*. The feeling of receiving a hard box, the unwrapping excitement, the way they showcase how their prints are drawn and how their products are made . . . just makes you go 'I want'.

I thought about this a lot, and for some reason, it kept me up at night.

How come no one had thought of that? How come everyone puts international brands on a pedestal? How come there was no Islamic or modest fashion brand that made people go 'Damn, I want'?

I wondered why not.

And at 2 a.m. on that one fine day in 2014, I started to wonder, *Why not me?*

That sleepless night turned into more sleepless nights as I couldn't stop thinking about this. I wanted to create an aspirational brand that celebrates and elevates the modest woman, Muslim or not. I wanted a brand that showed Muslim women as world travellers, stylish and confident goal-chasers. I wanted to create a brand that made Muslim women say 'I want!' and non-Muslim women say 'That's pretty cool'.

'We should do it!' Fadza said when I woke him up.

Not sure if it was because he was sleep-talking but the rest is history.

Starting with a Unique Concept

I penned down the idea I had and started working on a plan. What the brand needed, who to contact, who to hire, the works.

I wanted the name to be catchy. I was writing my blog, which I had named Proudduck, and the word 'duck' just stood out to me. It was easy to say, it was friendly, it was catchy, and it would definitely get people going 'Huh?' That last bit is important—the talkability of any brand is crucial. A brand called 'duck' selling scarves? That doesn't make sense at all. Just like how it doesn't make sense to sell gadgets and name your brand after fruit. Look where Apple is now.

I thought of packaging before product. The packaging is the first thing people see, and the first impression counts. I knew from the get-go that I needed this brand to have an awesome unboxing experience. It had to feel like opening a present. And the ultimate inspiration came to mind—Hermes. The way people swoon over the orange box, the way people stack their orange boxes as home décor—that orange box is iconic. I knew I wanted a square hard box, perfectly suited to house a folded scarf. I imagine people collecting these boxes and stacking them up to show off their collections. Little did I know they would do even more than that.

Learning from years of admiring Hermes, I knew I needed a statement colour. None of this white and black business—almost every brand plays safe with those. I needed a *colour*, preferably one that wasn't associated to a global brand yet. Hermes had orange, Tiffany & Co. had turquoise, Coca-Cola had red, Milo had green, Barbie had pink. I went through the colour chart and almost all the colours had been taken. My eyes fell on purple. I imagined it as a square box . . . hmmm, looks pretty delicious. The only big brand that came to mind using purple was Cadbury, one of my favourite chocolate brands. I didn't mind it, I imagined we'd be big enough one day to do a collaboration with them—dUCk chocolate (dark chocolate, geddit geddit?)

I googled the meaning of the colour purple: luxury, creativity, mystery, magical.

Ding, ding, ding! I think we have our colour.

Okay, so I've figured out the name, the packaging, the colour.

Yet somehow it still felt so . . . normal.

How do I push the envelope even further?

At that time, girls around the world were obsessed with the series *Gossip Girl*. Everyone wanted to be Serena Van Der Woodsen (but I'm totally #TeamBlair all the way). But the way the series was positioned was via a narration by this mystery narrator whom we only know as Gossip Girl. No one knew who she was, no one had seen her, but the entire series was her story to tell. To have the entire show narrated by someone mysterious was exciting—you never get to know Gossip Girl, but you couldn't wait to hear from her again. Was she Serena? Was she Blair? Was she Chuck Bass? I was too busy trying to keep my business afloat to finish watching the series (also it got too complicated; I couldn't keep up), so if Gossip Girl actually revealed herself in the end, DO NOT spoil it for me.

An idea sparked in me.

What if dUCk had a narrator? What if dUCk had a persona?—a girl who wears the hijab and is going through life, just like the rest of us. She would have a mom who nags her for not getting married yet, she would have boy issues, she would have best friends who have sleepovers with her till they're old, she would have happiness and regrets, just like us. I will call her D. I will not divulge here if D is a real person or based on a person, and if yes, whom. But I knew everyone would assume D was me, so I added a cat to the story. I would never get a cat. #DisnotVivy

Everything about the brand would be narrated by D. She would share her life stories and turn them into inspirations for her collections. I was always drawn to beautiful illustrations of chic and stylish women so I decided we would keep D's mystery by only showing her via lifestyle illustrations. Her working, her travelling, her going on a blind date, even her taking selfies—all these would be illustrated.

Brand persona D, sorted!

A Brand Can't Be for Everyone

Now, product positioning and pricing.

'That's the price you want to put?' Fadza asked, surprised when I told him.

At this point, we were just talking about the concept without any product details.

'Yeah, otherwise it would be too expensive and no one would buy,' I answered, worried.

'With that price, you'd be swimming with the rest of the brands out there,' Fadza advised.

He had a point. I would be entering a red sea if I priced it like everyone did. I knew customer behaviour—customers will like brands they feel they resonate with. Most customers are not rational buyers—if we were, luxury brands wouldn't exist. You don't buy a Rolex because you want a watch, you buy a Rolex because of the brand.

Sell a brand, not products. Just look at Supreme, Apple and the likes—they've created a brand so cool that it almost didn't matter what they launched because people want to have whatever they make. I needed dUCk to join this list of brands.

I knew dUCk was not going to be the brand for everyone—no brand is for everyone. Brands who say 'we are for everyone' have a huge burden on them because (a) how can you be something for everyone? And (b) it sounds like an expensive strategy to market to *everyone*. It's much easier to narrow down to a niche—have more clarity about who your customers will be.

Fadza and I looked at the different customer segmentation out there. As much as I'd like everyone to be a dUCk customer, I had to be real with myself—dUCk is more likely to attract a woman who lives in the city, has disposable income, likes designer brands and travelling. She is tech savvy, has a social media account and is attracted to aspirational photos. She is a woman on the go, and wants to look stylish throughout her day. She values friendship and goes on girlfriend trips to discover the world together. She cares less about gossip and more about doing good for others. That's why dUCk hardly does collaborations with celebrities; instead, we do more tie-ups with charity bodies and single moms. We went down to the details of where she would be dining, what her occupation would more likely be, is she a manager or is she an executive, is she a student or is she working—all these questions are so important to know who exactly the brand would speak to.

'Okay, what kind of price point do you think we should be aiming for?' I asked Fadza.

'Well, with the concept that you have in mind, it's most definitely a premium brand. You should be looking at this kind of price range,' he said showing me a number.

Whoa. It was triple of what the market generally offered.

'No one prices like that,' I told him.

'Exactly,' he said confidently.

I then thought about what more I could offer customers if I wanted to be in the premium segment—better quality, better packaging, better everything! I got super excited.

Okay then, price sorted!

That M Word Again

Money.

Funding-wise, we didn't have the money to launch this brand. FashionValet, the platform, had some, but it was needed to fund the platform business. A lot of people think we just pull money out of our bottoms, and quite honestly, I am past arguing with people who think 'Vivy Yusof has money falling from the sky'. Let people think what they want to think. But the truth was that dUCk was built from a loan that we had to pitch for—and no, there weren't any connections or 'backdoors' involved. There wasn't even a window, let alone a door.

No bank wanted to fund dUCk, because like I mentioned earlier in the book, no bank will fund an idea that has no track record. We were looking around for grants, but there weren't any. We could have asked our parents, but we didn't want to burden them.

Suddenly, one day, Fadza and I came across a news article that there was an investment firm called MyCreative that helped businesses in the creative industry, specifically. The article mentioned it was more for the arts, media, etc. and didn't mention fashion.

'But fashion is considered a creative industry, right?' I had to ask Fadza for confirmation.

'Let's find out,' he said.

Turns out, yes! If we didn't ask, we would have never found out.

Fadza took full charge of the pitch to them. He set up the appointment online and filled up all the forms. He had to do the concept deck with financial projections. We went to the first interview, nervous but passionate. They had some concerns, especially with the premium price of the dUCk scarves. I mean, it was unheard of back then. We had a few follow-ups, and finally, they agreed to fund it! It was a RM 300,000 loan, not a grant, so we would have to pay back with interest.

That's fine, we will work our butts off!

So we got to work like ducks—calm on the outside, but paddling like mad underneath the water.

Assembling the Team

We needed people to help us. The first person I called was my friend Shentel, the co-founder of accessories brands Sereni & Shentel and Bowerhaus. She is an amazing graphic designer who is full of ideas and her cheerful positivity just resonated with me and what I wanted dUCk to be. So I picked her brains for the logo and packaging.

It didn't take long for me to explain the brand concept to Shentel. She got it immediately and said, 'I love it. I can feel this will be big'. Her words of encouragement soothed me, and speaking to her got me even more excited as I waited eagerly for her design ideas. The moment her email came into my inbox, my fingers started shaking. I was so excited to meet my future logo and packaging, and I smiled when I first laid eyes on it. It's the same one you see today.

I assembled the pioneer team—a manager who would help me execute my ideas, a brand executive who would assist her and an intern. I literally went through my entire contacts list and also stalked some people on Facebook to find them. I also found a schoolmate of mine who could do illustrations, so I hired her to do the illustrations of D, since I can't draw to save my life.

The irony was that none of these ladies I hired wore the hijab. Two were Chinese and had never even touched a headscarf before.

'Are you sure I'm the right person for this?' they asked, shocked.

'Positive!'

I assembled this team on purpose, because I didn't want some hijab experts. Sometimes, when you hire experts, they get stuck in what they know and are unable to look at new perspectives. They will pour into your company what they've learnt from their previous companies, so in the end, you will *become* like their previous companies. I didn't want to create a brand that was already out there. My ambitions are bigger than that. I wanted to build something completely new. I wanted innovation and a fresh lens. I wanted a cool scarf brand that positioned the scarf differently than the rest. I think I was able to build dUCk the way I did *because* I didn't know a thing about the scarves market either.

And I loved the fact that none of these ladies knew what the heck a magic inner was either.

Creating Magic Together

'Okay, ready for the launch tomorrow?' my colleagues asked, excited.

I couldn't sleep that night. It was like setting up the FashionValet platform all over again. The excitement to launch, the anxiety of finding out people's reaction to it—the adrenaline just kept me awake as I reminisced the months leading up to that launch eve.

A few months prior to this day, I had gotten the first batch of scarves that I'd ordered. I went to a fabric shop to choose the fabric myself—a nice chiffon that fit our budget—and I got my friend's manufacturer to help me sew it up into shawls.

'The scarves are done! Delivering them over to you tomorrow,' the message from my friend made my day.

The boxes of scarves arrived at the office, and I ran to open them. Our first-ever batch of dUCk scarves. *I am so excited to meet you*, I mouthed silently as I lay my hands on the box. This was it. The contents of this box were going to be the debut of dUCk to the world.

The team and I huddled on the floor with scissors to open the boxes. There the scarves lay neatly, our first baby! The team squealed in delight, excited. They unfolded some of the scarves and gushed over the excitement to launch them.

I sat there silently.

'What's wrong?' they asked.

'This is not it. This isn't dUCk,' I replied, sombre.

Nothing was wrong with them, but they didn't wow me. The scarves looked like they were from any other brand out there—a normal chiffon scarf. That's it. That's not dUCk.

'But don't worry, we have the purple box and everything!' the team assured me.

'They're not going to walk around town with the purple box on their heads. The product itself has no wow factor. We can't use these,' I replied, disappointed as ever with myself because I was the one who chose them.

I had let the team down, but I stuck to my gut. And my gut told me this wasn't dUCk. Data can tell you chiffon scarves sell like hotcakes so please sell them, but data cannot tell you that if you sell these, you'll be just like everyone else.

So two problems I'd created for myself now.

Number one, what do we do with these hundreds of scarves that have arrived?

Number two, if this is not the dUCk scarf I envisioned, then what *is* a dUCk scarf?

We settled the first problem pretty fast by selling them on FashionValet platform under an unknown brand. Data told me chiffon scarves sell well, so true enough, they all sold out eventually. It didn't wow anybody, and no one remembers that brand, but it served the purpose—a simple chiffon scarf. We made back our money *and* FashionValet made commission, so phew.

For number two, I pondered a little longer. I stared at the dUCk logo that Shentel created. Hmmm. What if that little dUCk silhouette was on every scarf? Other brands typically sew a cloth label on the side of the scarf, but what if ours wasn't a normal label? What if ours was a charm, just a small one at the side, shining and glistening with every movement? Subtle luxury that gives off the 'if you know, you know' vibe. *That's hot*, I thought.

Okay but that's at the *end* of the scarf. If we take photos, people can only see the faces. Is there something that can be done that when you see the face, you immediately *know* someone was wearing a dUCk scarf? My memory brought me to this one Fendi scarf that I had— the two ends had some kind of comb-like hem that I thought was so elegant. But this was a luxury brand though. Could I pull it off? I shopped for manufacturers and finally found one that could do this particular hem finishing, which I later learnt was called 'picot hem' or 'eyelash hem'. Yes! When the sample arrived, I put it on and smiled.

Ah yes, this felt more like a dUCk scarf.

'Instead of the two ends only, let's do the hem all the way on every side,' I said.

'But the customer will have the hem all around her face when she wears the scarf,' the manufacturer said.

'Exactly,' I smiled.

'Won't that be too much?' she asked.

'Let's just do a sample and see.'

The samples came, and they were beautiful so we went all the way. The bulk order came after a couple of months, and we packed them. Neatly folded so the dUCk charm would face the customer when she opened the box. Wrapped in dUCk branded tissue paper, sealed with a dUCk sticker. The purple dUCk hard box housed them all, including an illustrated note from D to the customer. After that, each of the purple boxes was tied with dUCk-branded grosgrain ribbon.

Our QC process is very detailed. *Every* single piece of scarf goes through a QC process to check every hem, every charm and every inch—and this is something we do until today. While a lot of brands do random sampling QC method, we invest in a full QC to check every single piece to make sure our quality is never compromised.

It is a purple box of love.

As I reminisced about all this on the eve of launch, I was nervous but honestly, quite excited. After all the creative thought we'd poured into this debut, from product to packaging to marketing to branding, I was pretty confident that women out there would love it. My only worry was if people loved it enough to actually purchase it.

Well . . . WE. SOLD. OUT.

It was unbelievable, and we were left with two takeways. One, that there was an opportunity and a gap to be filled with a premium modest fashion brand. And two, that we were able to sell higher quantities all along! We could've been so much bigger had we controlled our supply earlier.

From that day in 2014 to 2021, dUCk has sold about three million pieces of scarves worldwide, and if we didn't try, we would have never known we were even capable of that.

Social Media Strategy

For many years, we really just focused dUCk's marketing efforts on social media. We didn't do any digital ads, billboards, TV ads, radio ads—none of that. Everything grew from social media, and it was free. If I ever meet Mark Zuckerberg, I would just give him a hug—because of the platform he created, many businesses around the world were able to grow. Apart from that, dUCk leveraged support from my reach on social media and FashionValet's pool of customers, since dUCk sold exclusively on FashionValet.

The strategy really revolved around storytelling. dUCk's social media was narrated by D, with captions in her voice with her illustrations that were relatable—her checking-in at the airport, her mom and her in the kitchen when her mom came to help her spring clean, even her standing on a chair at a café to take a food flatlay. I wanted women to scroll through dUCk's feed and go, 'That's me!' I wanted dUCk to connect women together with the little everyday things that we do and instantly feel like they were not alone.

I was so fussy with what I wanted for dUCk's Instagram page. The photos needed to be in natural lighting only, the sun's gotta be shining, there's gotta be pops of colours, women we repost should be enjoying life. I wanted dUCk's Instagram to be a woman's happy place, depicting the positive side of life—that life can be full of colour and smiles, if only we choose to see it that way. I wanted to be an advocate for that, via my brand—to uplift women with optimism for life. dUCk needed to be aspirational but friendly, which isn't an easy combination to build on because they were constrasting ideas.

I always tell the team even today, that dUCk is not about products alone, it's so much bigger than that. I wanted this brand to be about women and helping women rise—be it in their careers, in their families, in gaining more knowledge, in seeing the world or opening our eyes. So one thing I thought we could do was share our travels with the world. We would go to cities around the world, and do an Instagram takeover showing our followers all around the city. Not everyone has the privilege of travelling the world, so this way, we don't leave anyone behind. You don't know what Alhambra looks like? Let us go there and show you. Never looked up at the Eiffel tower? Let us be your eyes and show you. Never seen the inside of the Blue Mosque in Istanbul? Let us do the queuing up and show you.

With that travel element in mind, I wanted to connect it to a product. We would launch scarves with skylines on them, starting with Kuala Lumpur. It sold out in a matter of hours on the day of launch. Slowly, we released the same design but in new colours. Then we launched The Singapore dUCk, The London dUCk, etc. And each one was accompanied by an Instagram takeover of us travelling there. In the beginning, Fadza and I would be the ones going—him as the planner, photographer and scarves-ironer #haha; me as the model, makeup artist and hijab stylist. Most people take an entourage for these things, but Fadza and I wanted it to be more relatable—plus, we saved so much money. Imagine having to fly an entourage—the flight tickets, the hotel accommodation, travel expenses. But because we both had FashionValet work, too, these trips would be three days max.

We would arrive at the hotel, quickly prepare all the outfits, iron each one, and start the next day early with photoshoots. Usually, we would have two full days of shoot, and we would shoot an average of sixteen scarves in any one collection. That also meant sixteen different outfits. You'd laugh seeing us going from location to location, just the two of us, holding the perfectly ironed scarves on our arms and shoulders, and changing in the middle of the street for the next outfit. When it looked like it was going to rain, we'd rush like mad to complete all the looks before the outfits got wet. You'd never know all this from the Instagram posts, which were perfectly curated, with me smiling in the photos like a happy tourist. When really, in my head, I was thinking of the ten other outfits I needed to complete shooting before the rain came down. On the flights back to KL, I would be editing the photos and planning the storyline for social media.

Funnily enough, these work trips were always the most memorable. Challenging, but it was always an achievement when we'd complete the entire shoot and the travel content. It's made it feel even more worth it when we publish it on social media and our customers and followers appreciate them.

'I don't know when I will ever get to go, so thank you for taking us here.'

'Makes me feel like I just travelled the world with you.'

'This is exactly why I love dUCk.'

Comments like these flooded our social media and made my day. This was exactly what I wanted for a brand like dUCk. Not just to sell products, but to give some value to women everywhere.

From this travel element, we started the hashtag #ducktravels. And with this hashtag, our customers (who affectionately call themselves 'duckies') uploaded their own travel content. They'd go around the world bringing their purple dUCk boxes or wearing their dUCk scarf, and proudly sharing it using the hashtag. Another hashtag that went viral was #ducktower. Our customers would stack up their dUCk boxes into a tower, and it became a fun movement on Instagram to see how high your tower could get. Customers would collect the dUCk boxes and post on Instagram to share their #ducktower. Some would have dUCk towers all the way to the ceiling, some would measure it against their kids, some would have multiple towers by their bedside— it was something I've never seen before from any brand. I mean, this was all organic! Most brands would kill for this kind of community love and user-generated content. We didn't pay anyone to post like this, it was all by our beloved customers—the pride and connection they feel in relation to dUCk is something I'm just so grateful for.

For a few good years, I took all the photos and uploaded all the captions on dUCk's Instagram. Everything had to go through me. Every photo on the feed had to look a certain way. I'm ashamed to say I was incredibly protective of the branding to the point that I would not delegate it to anyone. Instagram was our only point of communication with the customers, I thought, so there was no way I could let anyone else handle that. People kept praising dUCk's branding, which validated everything we did, but that added to the pressure of me micromanaging even more, in fear of losing that special thing we had.

In hindsight, I know I didn't delegate it because I didn't want to. I loved doing it myself—I love social media, and I love the concept of dUCk to the point that I became obsessed.

'Can you put the phone away so you can actually *eat* your lunch?' Fadza would tell me.

We'd be at a nice café, and I would be more interested in taking photos of the food with the purple dUCk box in the frame.

'Huh? Oh yeah yeah, just a bit more, sorry,' I would reply to him as I finished writing the caption for dUCk's Instagram. Then, after I uploaded the picture, I would scroll through the comments and refresh to see if there were any new ones.

Looking back, I find it so horrible that I was like that, but you could also argue that obsession is needed to make something successful, especially in the early start-up days.

Everywhere I went, you would see a purple box peeping out from my handbag—just in case I wanted it for social media content.

I would stop at beautiful places and make Fadza take photos of me in the dUCk scarf. I would make him stop the car if I saw a nice wall that matched my scarf. As you can see, Fadza is an extremely patient man. #thankyoufornotleavingme. But he didn't mind, because he too wanted to do whatever it took to grow this special brand. He was always behind the scenes, helping me flip my scarf in photos so it would have that 'wind blowing' effect, and sometimes, he would even be our hand model in photos if we needed free help. dUCk became our lifestyle, and it honestly felt so natural to me. I never saw it as 'work' because I truly love the brand and what it stands for.

I would post several times a day on behalf of D, with whatever I felt like writing. There was no social media plan back then, because to me, it had to come from the heart. A detailed post schedule felt so clinical and not authentic. You can have a guide of what to talk about, but you need to listen to the customers in the comments section to know what they want to see or talk about. I listened very closely and let the customers guide me. It seemed to work because we had one of the most engaged Instagram accounts, and very quickly rose to hundreds of thousands of followers in a short amount of time.

But of course, it was easier back then. There was only the Instagram post. Now, the list never ends with Instagram post, stories, reposts, direct messages, lives, reels, shop features, and God knows what else they will roll out. NFTs? Even in the Story function alone, there are many features to use—gifs, links, polls, quizzes etc. And that's *just* Instagram—we haven't even talked about Facebook, Twitter, TikTok and other platforms I don't even dare to download. It's way too noisy now, and I really do empathize with whoever handles social media content for brands. You guys deserve medals. It's not an easy portfolio to have, especially because there is just so much content out there fighting for customers' attention.

So to any of you reading this and starting brands on social media, I can understand if you're stressed because there seems to be so much to do. But all I can say is it's important to stay true to yourself. If something doesn't feel natural to you or the brand, don't do it. Don't follow trends if it doesn't suit your brand. Don't be pressured to join the pack. People can see right through the inauthenticity, so you do you but be consistent.

Keeping Up the Hype

No amazing marketing can sustain a brand's success if your products are crappy. Maybe customers will buy once, but they will never come back. Knowing that, from Day One, I obsessed over the quality of dUCk products. I didn't settle on the first batch that arrived; I did whatever I could to salvage the situation and recover the cost of that mistake.

Today, we have a full-blown team who are fabric specialists but back then, it was little old me choosing the fabrics that would potentially become dUCk scarves. I would sit on the floor with a whole pile of fabric and try them on one by one, checking the thickness, the flow of the material, the opacity, the crease levels, everything. I had no idea about fabric, but I just put myself in the customer's shoes and asked a simple question: 'Would our customers wear this?' I might not be a specialist, but it wasn't rocket science.

What was shocking to us was that we found out there was a secondary market for dUCk. We would launch collections, they would sell out fast and people would see this as an opportunity to resell the scarves for a profit. Resellers would buy the scarf for the usual retail price of RM 300 on launch day, and resell it for RM 1,500 because the demand would be really high. They were making more margins than us!

The demand for limited-edition dUCk collections would be so high that we would sell out in minutes online, and then we would see queues as early as 5 a.m. at the dUCk stores. Before we had stores, we would open booths at bazaars, but we soon outgrew that. We would have metres-long queues, which upset other vendors because the queue would be blocking their booths from the public. Our sales assistants would also get asked if they could sell the piece they were wearing on their heads. It got so bad that our customers got angry with the constant sold-out status, so we resorted to limiting purchase

quantity to only one scarf per customer. We had to put limits on how
many a person could buy—it was unbelievable! And pretty soon, we
saw another challenge—counterfeits! Because it was so scarce in the
market, people took advantage and produced fake versions of our
products; annoyed is an understatement for how we all felt. But more
of this in Chapter 12.

This is what happens when you have the scarcity element where
there are only limited quantities. When there's scarcity, there's hype.
But another challenge is how do you keep that scarcity or hype *and*
grow? If you stay scarce, your revenue won't grow and your number
of customers won't grow. Only a limited number of people are able to
buy and wear, and there is loss of opportunity because the brand could
have sold more. We learnt to balance over the years—some collections
had to be limited to keep the brand special, but the core products had
to be in stock at all times. It's a tough balance, of course, because
there's always that temptation to make more quantities because you
can make more revenue for the company. So someone has to keep it
disciplined; most of the time in our case, it was Fadza.

Another way we kept up the hype is via collaborations.

With dUCk's quick rise, offers came from many brands to
collaborate, but I wanted to keep dUCk a bit more exclusive. It was
so tempting to just say yes to everyone, and I wanted to at times, but
I had to think long term. dUCk cannot be seen as a brand that would
collaborate with just anyone and they had to be never-been-done-
before collaborations.

One fine day in Brunei, we were doing our Eid pop-up for
FashionValet. I was there meeting customers and showing them all
the brands on FashionValet, and was in full-on salesperson mode.
Suddenly, we got a message from the hotel that the Crown Princess of
Brunei wanted to visit. I panicked. Brunei royalty are extremely private
and exclusive, so this was a rare moment. I was flattered, but I couldn't
even think about that at the time.

She arrived, elegant and poised. She was soft-spoken and smiled
at everyone. I was so nervous next to her, but I tried my best to be

as well-behaved as I could. I showed her around and she chose some items to purchase. And that was that.

Wouldn't it be cool if we could collaborate with her? Now that's something the world hasn't seen. A crown princess who wears a hijab, collaborating with a hijab brand.

'Don't be ridiculous, Vivy, she'll definitely say no,' my logical side, the left brain, snapped.

'You'll just embarrass yourself,' it kept going.

Then my right brain snapped back, 'This could be the one-of-a-kind collaboration you've always wanted.'

My heart agreed. 'If you don't ask, you'll forever wonder "What if?"'

That was all I needed.

'Umm, Pr—Prince—Princess Sarah,' I stuttered. 'Would you be open to a collaboration with dUCk?'

She smiled but didn't say anything. I was a ball of nerves then, so I can't even remember the exact thing that happened next. But all I knew was that we said our goodbyes and I thought that was the last I would see of her. And I wanted to go back to my hotel room and kick myself in the head.

Soon after, we got a message that the Crown Princess was keen to have a further discussion. I couldn't believe it. Fast forward to months later, we launched a never-done-before collaboration between dUCk and Her Royal Highness The Crown Princess of Brunei, Princess Sarah. It was news both in Brunei and in Malaysia, as she was loved by both nations. We had a launch event in Brunei with people so excited to see her that the collection sold out in no time on FashionValet, and we were left with a surge of new Bruneian customers.

It gives me goosebumps to think what I would have missed had I kept my mouth shut on that one fateful day.

Soon, international brands took notice. We had our next big collaboration with Disney, and we were not only the first modest fashion brand to do so, but also the first local brand in Malaysia. It was very well-received by our customers. Then we collaborated with other global names like Barbie, Marvel, Baskin Robbins and Starbucks—

and we were the first modest fashion brand to break that glass ceiling. Our beauty line made dUCk one of the first halal beauty brands to enter Sephora. One collaboration close to my heart was Monopoly x dUCk, where we created a special dUCk-themed Monopoly board game, which became the first Monopoly that had a hijabi on it. Proud would be an understatement for what we felt on the day it all sold out. Collaborating with these global names was just a dream of mine before. Who would have thought a small brand from Malaysia could get the attention of these global names? *Barbie was part of my childhood memories, now I'm collaborating with them? I used to watch Mickey Mouse on TV, and now I'm collaborating with Disney?* It just proved to me that dreams do come true.

The challenge now is to keep on innovating, and it gets harder because nowadays you see brands collaborating left, right and centre in this fast-paced era. Nothing is one-of-a-kind any more, and it's every brand's challenge to figure out their own journey. Stay tuned for dUCk's!

Mistakes and Conflicts

As much as we had a lot of love for our products and collaborations, we were not free from mistakes either. Some collections were misses and they stay vivid in my mind to remind me to not repeat those.

One that I remember was the World Map dUCk collection. It was a printed scarf with the world map design and little dUCk silhouettes peppered all over, depicting us dUCkies travelling the world together. The colour combinations were so beautiful, everyone loved it—in a matter of minutes, the World Map dUCk sold out. We were thrilled that customers loved it.

'Oh my god,' one of the team members exclaimed suddenly, looking at her phone.

'What, what?' We all gathered.

We were crushed at what we saw. A customer had pointed out on social media that the names of the countries were printed a few centimetres off the map, which means the countries weren't labelled accurately. Even Kuala Lumpur was not tagged as Kuala Lumpur.

If a child learnt geography from the World Map dUCk, he would fail his exams for sure. From that one post, the news spread so fast and people started sending complaints to us. People even made fun of us, saying that we were sleeping when labelling the countries and the dUCk team probably skipped geography classes in school. To be fair, they were not wrong—Geography was my least favourite subject.

It was embarrassing, and we had to take accountability for this. We spoke to our supplier to reprint the scarves immediately and negotiated a one-month timeline—it was so rushed but we begged them. We stayed up in the office matching every country to the name and our designer made the changes immediately. Everyone was in intense let's-save-this mode.

We made an announcement that we would send each customer a new World Map dUCk scarf for free, one that was corrected. That meant thousands of free scarves *and* delivery costs. We didn't trouble the customers by recalling the faulty ones, plus the shipping costs we would have to bear would be so much. So we let every customer keep the original scarf.

It was a dent in our financial books and a dent in our premium image. I was thinking, 'My god, why didn't we check?' and beating myself up about it. What's worse was that I was in the public eye so people made fun of me for not knowing where countries are. I accepted the hit, but eventually, we all had to move on. We made a booboo, we fixed it, now let's learn never to do it again. From then on, we never took product design for granted. We check and test everything till today, in fear of disappointing our customers again. Oddly enough, this mistake made our customers love us even more. They applauded the way we handled the mistake and how we took steps to apologize and rectify it. It made me realize that customers are human beings, too—they are forgiving and they see your efforts to make things right.

(Fun fact: The wrongly labelled scarf was then seen as a rare item and was sold at even higher prices in the secondary market. It was seen as more valuable than the correct one!)

Another booboo we made was a product in our Marvel Ironman collaboration. It was in conjunction with Father's Day, so we made the theme 'I love you 3000', the famous line that Tony Stark's daughter said to him. We wanted to signify the love between a daughter and her father, so we needed a men's product. We decided to go with a silk tie, in line with our premium offerings. Even before we launched it, we got some backlash on social media—someone pointed out that Muslim men are not allowed to wear silk. I knew that, but me and my product team completely missed it, and I was so embarrassed. I guess we always see silk ties being sold by luxury brands like Hermes and Louis Vuitton, and I see Muslim men wear those without a second thought, so it didn't come up as a red flag to me. But the bottom line is we had a responsibility as a brand; I had a responsibility to my religion and I was at fault. We stopped the selling of these silk ties immediately and instead decided to gift them all to non-Muslim male frontliners in hospitals who were working tirelessly to combat COVID-19.

And there were many more booboos that we learnt from. It's important to note that while we faced backlash at the time, none of these mistakes stopped us from growing further. It's true when people say that we can only grow from our mistakes. Learn from them and move on.

I am jumping forward in the timeline now. The trust that our customers put in us helped grow the brand, slowly but surely. Over the years, we released more collections and expanded to other categories as well. From scarves, we did cosmetics, bags, home and living, and ready-to-wear. In 2021, we launched a kids' line too, and aptly called it dUCkling. We tested with a small experimental launch and everything sold out in a day! Even today, I get butterflies whenever I spot someone wearing a dUCk, or see purple paper bags being carried all over malls. The love from our customers is something I don't take for granted, and it's precisely because of them that we are still standing today.

Marketplaces came knocking on our doors, wanting us to stock with them, but I politely declined. dUCk was to be sold on FashionValet only; I stayed firm on that. dUCk had the ability to bring traffic to the brand, so I needed to keep that traffic coming to the FashionValet website instead of other sites. Both of them were under the same group anyway, so they needed to help each other. You'll see why this became a problem, later in the book.

dUCk didn't just fill the gap in modest fashion; what people didn't know was that dUCk kept FashionValet alive. dUCk was subsidizing FashionValet financially, and pretty soon, Fadza and I would be facing a big conflict.

Chapter 9

The Dilemma

But first, back to FashionValet.

The vision was simple and clear.

FashionValet would be the hub for Southeast Asian fashion designers and brands.

We would carry the best of Malaysian designers and brands (including our own ones), and then Indonesian designers and brands, and then Thai designers and brands, and so on. It would be the one-stop hub for Asian fashion and each country's local designers, a place where people could discover culture through fashion. Customers would come primarily from the countries the designers were from, out of patriotism, and eventually, they would discover the other selections on the website. Investors loved this, as we didn't just focus on Malaysian growth. Our ambition was global domination from the start, proudly carrying the Asian flag.

The reality?

Sips tea

Growing a business in your own country is hard enough. Growing a business in another country is at a whole other level of 'why the fruit am I doing this again?' It is tough and incredibly humbling. You will have the home advantage on your own turf because you know the ins and outs, and people might want to support you simply because you're homegrown. In a foreign land, you have to start from ground zero and there's no obligation from others to pay attention to you.

We tried to expand into the Indonesian market. In the early days, we tested the waters with bloggers first, because we needed help to spread the word about us. This was in the pre-Instagram days. We found that the most famous Indonesian fashion blogger at the time was this super cool girl called Diana Rikasari (this was years before we created a brand with her). There was an email address on her blog so okay, let me just build up the courage to contact her. I needed my email to stand out because, of course, she got a tonne of emails a day.

'Dear Diana,' I began and drafted the email. I needed to sound like a super fan but I couldn't sound too desperate. Wanted to sound cool, but not *too* cool. Wanted her to see the excitement of the platform, but needed to make sure it didn't come off as too needy.

Argh, just do it, Vivy. Say Bismillah and let's go! I clicked Send Email.

Days later, I almost fell off my chair when she replied. She was open to reviewing some of the things on FashionValet, she chose some things with the store credit we gave her and we kissed the box before it took its journey to Indonesia.

It felt like years waiting to hear back from her. I remember refreshing her blog every day to see if she'd posted about us. Nothing. I contacted her, and it turned out that the parcel was not only slow to arrive, Diana also had to pay a high tax for it. That was the first red flag: cross-border shipments.

There were other obstacles that were just tapping their fingers, waiting for us to arrive. But first, let me take you to the beginning—our first sip from the 'international' cup.

Hello, Indonesia

It started with a trip to Jakarta in 2012.

I was preparing for my wedding (I mean, *our* wedding) and decided to get a lot of the things from Indonesia—the invitation cards, the door gifts, even my wedding dress. I had been to Jakarta a few times prior to this, but this time I was an entrepreneur. Which means anywhere you go, you will think, 'Is there a business opportunity here? Could I do something here?' You live and breathe your business 24/7. It happens naturally and there's nothing you can do to switch it off.

I wanted to check out the malls to see the fashion there, and Asma' came with me. We were both mesmerized by what we discovered. Not only did Indonesia have way more designers and variety, they also had a whole floor dedicated to them in Plaza Senayan called Level One. It was a strip in the mall fully dedicated to promoting their local brands, and I wondered why there wasn't anything like that in Malaysia.

They had at least twenty stores along the strip, and each store was decorated so beautifully. They looked like international brands, each bursting with fashion creativity and a unique retail experience. Asma' and I looked at each other, our eyes big with excitement.

'Are you thinking what I'm thinking?' we asked each other.

Get Indonesian brands on FashionValet!

We went into full work mode. We walked from store to store, checking out the clothes and asking for the manager's contact details. We split the strip—I took left, Asma' took right. By the end of it, we had got the business cards and so many lookbooks that we needed a bag *just* for those. We went for lunch but it wasn't to eat. It was to sit down somewhere so we could make calls to these phone numbers. I can't speak Indonesian fluently, but I tried anyway—as long as they understood me, I was good. We had two days left in Jakarta so we challenged ourselves to pack them with meetings to sign on the brands.

I wasn't sure what was more exciting about that trip—my wedding preparations or signing on Indonesian local brands. Asma' and I managed to sign a lot of brands there on that trip, and it was crazy that we even managed to take back stock immediately from a few of those brands. Our suitcases, coming back, were full with stock and we couldn't wait to tell the team that we now had Indonesian brands on FashionValet.

From then on, 'Mission Indonesia' was *on*.

Asma' and I went for Indonesian Fashion Weeks, which were the best platforms for us to discover many local brands at once. They not only had the runways for the shows, but more importantly, they had booths for every local brand where they displayed their designs. This was amazing for us because we got to speak to the designer directly without wasting time. There were floors full of these booths and hundreds of brands to see. Overwhelming, for sure, but Asma' and I were young and pumped. We had a folder of empty consignment contracts ready to be signed, a tonne of our name-cards and iPads to show the brands our website. I can't remember if we even ate proper meals because there was so much to do and so little time. We had to talk to hundreds of brands within a deadline, so we were talking so fast from booth to booth, high on our own adrenaline rush.

By that time, people had heard of FashionValet in the Indonesian fashion industry. So it became easier to convince their designers and brands to join. We were the trusted Malaysian platform for local brands, and because their fashion peers had joined, they wanted to join too. It's just in the nature of human beings to have that FOMO, which worked really well for us.

Soon, we had over a hundred Indonesian brands on FashionValet, and we were even making exclusive collaborations with some of them. It was exciting! Variety on our website increased and customers were happy. Indonesian brands' items were also cheaper than most Malaysian brands, so they sold really well on our site. It was cheaper to go there and pick up a lot of stock ourselves than to ship heavy boxes internationally, so our trips to Jakarta became more frequent. Soon, we brought extra suitcases on every trip and even had to bring extra colleagues along just so we could have more suitcases.

We hired our first-ever employee in Jakarta, who was the Country Manager, Windy. She was well-connected within the industry with brands and influencers, and she was passionate about growing FashionValet in Indonesia. With the growing number of Indonesian brands on our site, it was no longer possible to fly back and forth to transport stock by hand. We opened up a company in Indonesia and we started to look at this expansion more seriously.

Asma' and I took a back seat, and from then on, the buyers took over. The number of brands signed grew and the stock received multiplied. To save cost, we decided to stop bringing stock back to Malaysia; we would carry out operations and fulfilment from our small and humble office-cum-warehouse in Jakarta. Photoshoots were done from there, and photos would be sent over along with the linesheets. Inventory from Indonesian brands was kept in our Jakarta warehouse. This meant that customers who ordered from Malaysia would get their Indonesian items a few days later. It was not ideal, but it was the most cost-efficient. The stocks were on consignment, so whatever was unsold would have to be shipped back to the brand—this meant many cross-border shipments being sent back and forth, which would be expensive and inefficient. It was the best option at the time, but it compromised the speed of delivery to our customers. Luckily for us, the customers didn't mind back then.

We were also getting noticed by the equivalents of FashionValet over there, but it wasn't a problem. Brands and designers loved the idea of working with FashionValet because of one thing—it was the door for them to expand their brands further to the Malaysian market. Our customers embraced the Indonesian brands on FashionValet, and demand for them increased.

It was great on the surface, but internally, it did not look good for us.

'International expansion isn't as lucrative as we thought,' Fadza and I would discuss and try to find solutions, leaving our dinner cold on the table.

In terms of costs and operations, it really complicated things for us. Single orders that had both Malaysian and Indonesian items had to be split and separated because they were being shipped by two different warehouses in different countries. Customers grew confused about why items were arriving at different times despite us notifying them in advance, and costs increased for us, obviously, because of the double shipments. We tried to negotiate with courier companies, but our volume just couldn't justify them giving us more discounts. It started to not make sense financially, but we powered through, treating it as a long-term investment into the Indonesian market. 'Nothing happens overnight, we have to invest some money to build our presence,' we reminded ourselves.

So we burnt a bit of money while waiting for the Indonesia customer database to grow on FashionValet. We had the Indonesian brands, surely, the Indonesian customers will slowly come too, right?

But they never did.

I could count the number of Indonesian customers we had on my hand.

Truth was, we were just growing *Malaysian* customers rapidly. Where were all the *Indonesian* customers?

We tried so many things. We did collaborations; we hired influencers; we held events; we did digital ads, we even did a pop-up store once, at one of the busiest malls in Jakarta. Our Indonesian customer base grew so slowly, we started getting concerned. Was this Southeast Asian fashion website a feasible idea at all? Are we just not doing it right? Was there something we were missing?

In hindsight, there were so many things we had to consider when going international, and so many of them we had missed. In no particular order, some of them are:

1. The website wasn't optimized to suit the local market. We had default currency of IDR whenever Indonesians went on it, but it still felt like a Malaysian website with the look and feel of the banners.

2. Shipping was too expensive, and custom charges were not friendly. We did a test of 'Free Shipping to Indonesia' and it increased our orders but then these orders got stuck in customs, and the customers had to pay taxes that were higher than the items themselves. They never came back.

3. Indonesians didn't need to buy Malaysian fashion brands. They have a huge pool of talented designers of their own. So there was no need or desire for them to own Malaysian designer pieces unless it was really one-of-a-kind stuff.

4. At that time, Indonesians preferred other shopping methods
    like physical stores and Whatsapp orders. It was very much
    a mall lifestyle. I'd been told that because the traffic was so
    bad there, they tended to stay in one mall and hold all their
    meetings and outings there. They also liked the human touch,
    so Whatsapp was a huge revenue driver and we failed to adapt
    fast at the time to this social commerce.

5. There were already equivalents of FashionValet there, some
    of the big ones being Zalora Indonesia and Hijup. We
    had the USP of being slightly more international, having
    catered to the markets of Malaysia, Singapore, and Brunei
    as an added bonus—which was attractive for the Indonesian
    designers who wanted to expand, but not for the Indonesian
    customers because they had little interest in non-Indonesian
    designers.

These are just some.

I haven't even included the different sets of business laws and
cultural differences that made everything harder.

And you're welcome, I just gave you a list of 'Things to Consider'
as you expand your own business.

It all happened so fast that as entrepreneurs, we just dove in.
Especially me being the *now* kind of girl: the waiting and researching
and thinking kills my momentum—just being honest. How much
market research was enough market research? Nothing is guaranteed.
Even companies with a whole thesis of market research still fail, so let's
just dive in and figure it out along the way, I would say at the time. I
can't say that if we did even more strategizing, it would have succeeded
because the biggest reality was that the market didn't want the product
we offered. It failed first and foremost because there was no product–
market fit. No one outside of Malaysia wanted or needed our platform
of local brands, and that's the reality of it. We were excited about
Indonesia, but Indonesia wasn't excited about us. At the same time, we
were trying to grow bigger in Malaysia, too, so we found ourselves not
focused, and often, exhausted.

Personally, I was caught up in the excitement and glamour of wanting to expand internationally, so much so that I didn't even think that was a question to consider. The arrogance of 'of course they would want my product, my product is awesome!' which lies at the heart of every passionate entrepreneur.

This was the reality of my journey, full of ups and downs, of achievements and mistakes. But I never stopped trying or learning: making mistakes sucks, of course, but had I not gone through this, I wouldn't have learnt all this. It's just so different living it yourself compared to reading a business textbook or listening to mentors' journeys. And because I've felt the pain, I'm careful to not be so hasty the next time.

So when you want to expand internationally, first question to ask yourself is, 'Would this country even want my product?'

And don't ask your mother. She'll always say yes because she's biased and she loves you. #iloveyoutooMom

Leaving Indonesia

The decision to close down our Indonesian operations was not easy. It was our first *big* failure and facing it personally was tough enough, but now telling the team was even more daunting.

How do you even begin to look your colleagues in the eye and say, 'I'm sorry but I'm taking away your job'? Not in those words, obviously, but no matter how you flower it up, that's what they will hear.

The management, including myself and Fadza, flew to Jakarta to deliver the news. On the plane, I was already tearing up. I was imagining the faces of our teammates, and my heart sank. They were good people and these are the moments in leadership when you feel like you don't deserve to lead.

The team had already known that we were not profitable in Indonesia and we were losing money, and they told me later that they had a feeling this was going to happen since all of us had come. The saddest part was that they had prepared a presentation on a complete rebrand that they wanted to do, that they wanted to present to Fadza and me. Our hearts broke because as much as we wanted to say yes, we knew that we had already made a decision and had a duty to our shareholders to stick to it. This was one of the hardest moments for me in my leadership journey, and I'm sure it was for Fadza too.

We did whatever we could after that; we stayed on to speak to every member of the team privately. We gave them a severance package and tried our best to help them get a job to move on to. It was the first time I saw Windy cry, and we hugged each other so tight that it really felt like my heart had shattered into pieces. This was her baby as much as it was ours, and we both apologized to each other for letting each other down. It was an emotional day, and I think everyone was silent all the way back to Malaysia. We just did not know what to say.

Years have passed by now, and it's still bittersweet. I'm proud that we took risks and gave it our all. And I realized failures do not kill you—hey, we are all still standing! It will suck for a while but when you're done hating yourself, you'll realize there's a rainbow at the end of the road. We all learnt valuable lessons that we could never have learnt anywhere else, and we forged friendships for a lifetime. Everyone in the team moved on to other jobs pretty quickly, much to my relief, because the loss of their future income was the one thing that kept me up at night during those days.

As for us, the closure helped us return our focus to our core market.

The Same Question Again

At some point in our journey, we dabbled in the Middle East too. In just a couple of months, we had traffic coming into the website from the region. Saudi, Kuwait, Qatar, Dubai—we were so excited. We ran ads and engaged modest fashion influencers. We even had a big launch there, where we brought five designers along to showcase in a fashion exhibition in Dubai. I remember it being so hot, around 40 degrees Celsius, and the team had to stand by the booth in the hot sun from morning till night. My day was packed with interviews and meetings, and I even gave a talk at a social media conference in

Dubai in front of 2,000 people. I was pregnant with my third child, Sarah, at the time, and I remember being so nervous I didn't know if I had to puke because of the talk or because of Sarah. Probably both.

It was a whole different ballgame there. The salary, first and foremost, was scary to us but this was the norm we had to accept. People in the Middle East get paid a lot more than Malaysians, maybe because the standard of living is much higher. When I first heard the salary bracket for even fresh graduates in Dubai, I needed to sit down and drink water. The cost of doing business there was so high compared to Southeast Asia, and it was something I wasn't used to but I had to swallow. If I wanted to go global, I'd got to think bigger. I'd have to think in US Dollars. I had to stop myself from converting to Malaysian Ringgit at every meeting because if I didn't stop, I would get panic attacks.

The cost would be justified if you consider that the people in the Middle East generally have bigger spending power. Their average basket value on the website was much higher than that of our Malaysian customers, so we knew that if we wanted to expand globally, Middle East needed to be on our radar.

But despite the traction we had, it all went back to that same question again. 'Does this country want my product?'

The answer was a big no.

Us: We have an amazing array of local brands from Southeast Asia!

Middle Easterners: That's nice. And . . ?

Painful, but this was the truth.

At the end of the day, it was like a company coming to us saying, 'We have a whole line-up of African/German/Mexican brands on this website. Come check it out!' We would probably be like, 'Huh, why?' No matter how nice the brands are, it just would not have any relation to us. This was exactly what was happening to FashionValet, the platform.

This also made me learn a painful business lesson: if you want to build a global brand, don't pigeonhole yourself to patriotic products. Patriotic products such as FashionValet could only work in that one country, that's all. Growth opportunities beyond that would be extremely slim.

This realization had always been deep in my heart when we started trying to go international, but I wanted to prove everyone wrong. I went against my gut, shh-ed the voices in my head and still talked about how amazing Southeast Asian brands are to the world. To whoever was willing to listen. Even the Uber driver in Dubai, who was so sweet to entertain me. He didn't buy anything from us, but still, very sweet man.

At the end of the day, product–market fit is very important. You must sell a product that the market wants. If you have to convince/beg/educate people who aren't even that interested, chances are you're not going to go far with that business.

The 'FashionValet or dUCk' Dilemma

At the same time, something weird was happening to us.

When our Middle East and North Africa (MENA) country manager Noor and team reached out to influencers, they kept asking about dUCk. They had not much to say about FashionValet, but a lot to say about dUCk.

'I've heard of it!'

'I've seen it on Instagram!'

'They don't ship here, do they?'

'I love the brand; my friends and I stalk it on social media.'

We kept sending FashionValet packages to them filled with products from the various brands we carried, but their interest always went back to dUCk.

It got confusing for the team because this revelation questioned our strategy. Budget had been allocated, and we were seeing traction, although slower than we expected. Here we were trying to expand FashionValet to the Middle East (and dUCk as *one* of the brands under it), but would we have grown a lot faster if we marketed dUCk as a single brand going to the Middle East? Would we have made better use of our expansion money if it was dUCk that we pushed, and not FashionValet?

Phrase of the day if you're starting a business: PRODUCT–MARKET FIT!

Now underline that three times.

I've never talked about this conflict on social media, but it was one that haunted me for years.

I've now created a brand that has become the heart and soul of FashionValet and is the reason we can still pay everyone's salary. But I was still the face of local brands—I had to talk about every brand on FashionValet and I, of course, wanted to do it fairly. I wanted to promote them equally. But here is dUCk, ready to fly even higher, and I had to say, 'Shh, don't make so much noise, we don't want to ruffle any feathers'. Deep inside, I knew that I'd not seen any brand grow on FashionValet the way dUCk was growing—I was so proud of it yet I felt so guilty about it. I wanted to grow dUCk to its fullest potential, but I was fearful of being seen as a traitor to other local brands. *You're supposed to promote us, not your own brand*, I imagined the voices telling me. And so I did both, in constant conflict, and it drove me nuts, mentally and physically.

It's not easy being the face of the brand. When things are good, it's great! But when there are problems (and there will be *many* problems), you are always the one accountable and you've got to face that publicly. You get called names, you get ridiculed and cancelled, whatever that actually means. At the same time, you've got to keep a pretty picture of your company before all stakeholders (your followers, your employees, the media) so it gets tiring to always keep that smile on your face. *Just smile, deal with it after this media interview. Just smile, deal with it after you post that happy thing on Instagram.*

People have told me that some brand owners (not all) felt resentful of dUCk, though I can't verify this. I was told that I don't promote their brands enough, or I don't take enough OOTDs of their clothes. I tried my best to serve all the brands, but it's impossible to take photos of hundreds of brands' products when you're one person with one body and one face. At the same time, I had this brand that was flourishing and that I felt *guilty* to promote. My team would say, 'Vivy, tonight there's the new dUCk product launch. Don't forget to post it on Instagram,' and I would say, 'No, no. Just let dUCk post about it. I need to promote FV, not dUCk.' In my heart, I knew by doing this, I was not being fair to dUCk.

One night, I was invited to a dinner with women leaders in Kuala Lumpur, hosted by our Governor. The VIP of the night was Christine Lagarde, the IMF Chairman at the time on her visit to our country. It was a big deal. I was sitting at a long dining table among women icons like our first female Deputy Prime Minister Dato' Seri Wan Azizah, ex-Governor Tan Sri Zeti Aziz and many others, and I had to compose myself from bursting into fangirl mode throughout the night. But one thing happened that night that I can never forget. When Christine Lagarde came to shake my hand, her tall stature towering over me, she gave me a big smile and said, 'Ah you're Vivy, the scarf girl.' I just returned her smile, not able to say a word. I left the dinner that night thinking, 'But no . . . I'm Vivy, the *FashionValet* girl.'

That night, I was representing FashionValet. In fact, every day I was representing FashionValet. But people still associated me most with dUCk scarves. Everywhere I went, people kept pushing dUCk to me no matter how hard I pushed FashionValet to them.

dUCk > FashionValet

I remember when we first dabbled in physical retail.

In 2015, we experimented with offline retail for FashionValet. There was an opportunity to open a pop-up store in Bangsar Village Mall, and we wanted to try it out. We thought it was a great idea to let people touch and feel the products from local brands, instead of just trying to suss them out from their computer screens. Never before was I so excited to open a store—we stayed till the wee hours of the night setting up railing and steaming out the creases from clothes and scarves from local brands. We sectioned the pop-up store by brand, so customers could experience each local brand as a whole.

What started as an experiment turned out to be a hit. I realized then the importance of having physical presence and not just relying on ecommerce. There is nothing tech can do to replace that feeling of walking through a store, touching the fabrics of gorgeous clothes, trying them out for yourself to see what size fits best. With the rise of ecommerce (especially with brands being forced to go online because of COVID-19), the online scene will get even more crowded, so it's even more important to balance it out with physical presence. We ramped up stores quickly and learnt that it was completely a different ballgame to the ecommerce life we were used to. We never had to worry about creases on display clothes, we never had to be face to face with a customer, we never had to deal with lines at cashiers and getting nervous that customers had to wait with frowns on their faces.

After years behind a screen in a warehouse, it was a whole new terrifying but exciting world dabbling in physical retail. Till today, I love going to the stores and talking to customers because you get to see the actual people who love your products. You get to ask them what you can do better. You get to hug them! And oh gosh, that feeling when you see people in malls carrying your paper bags—it makes every pain of running a business SO WORTH IT.

We continued to open more FashionValet stores, and we started approaching the A-malls in town. It was extremely difficult to get a spot in these malls, especially if you're a local brand. It's much better now, but back then, the leasing teams wouldn't even look at local brands. They only responded to the ZARAs and Uniqlos and Nikes of the world. It was almost unheard of for local brands to get any response, and you'd just stay on the waitlist forever. 'Try anyway!' I'd tell my team. If you don't try, you'll never know.

And what do you know, an A-mall in the heart of the city responded to our emails!

I did a little dance.

I stopped dancing when I found out they didn't want to offer a lot to FashionValet.

They wanted to offer a lot . . . to dUCk.

Umm . . . what?

I clarified. 'This lot is for a FashionValet store, right?'

'Uh, we can discuss an opportunity for FashionValet later, but we'd like to offer dUCk a lot. It's available now if dUCk is interested.'

'But I called for FashionValet . . .'

'Well, we noticed that you opened a booth at a Ramadhan bazaar recently and the lines were all the way to the entrance. We were very impressed, and we want that kind of traffic in our malls.'

'Um . . . but is there a lot for FashionValet too?'

Conversations like these happened often with mall managements. No matter how I sold FashionValet, what they wanted was dUCk. It felt like I was cheating on myself . . . with myself. It was such a weird feeling.

If dUCk opened stores of its own, what will happen to FV stores? The company would have to open two stores in the same mall, and both stores would stock dUCk items. Does that even make sense? Since we knew from our data that most people come to FashionValet for dUCk, not stocking dUCk in FashionValet stores would be a suicidal move for FashionValet.

And the dilemma wasn't just about retail spaces in shopping malls. It soon became about everything.

Can dUCk have its own website? Oh, no no, dUCk has to sell *under* FV.

Can dUCk have its own separate app? Oh, no way, dUCk must only sell *within* the FV app.

Can dUCk have a loyalty programme? No, FV already has one anyway.

Can this dUCk collection launch on Tuesday? No, sorry, this other brand has a big launch on FV. Change dUCk's date.

We laid so much importance on FashionValet and always being fair to other local brands that we totally suppressed dUCk's potential. dUCk constantly had to give in to FashionValet, and it was so silly because dUCk is literally owned *by* the FashionValet Group! I owed it to my company to make sure dUCk succeeded to its fullest potential. But I also owed it to my company to make sure FashionValet succeeded to its fullest potential. And at that time, that meant tying dUCk's hands and confining it to sell only through FashionValet. If there was a Facebook relationship status between the two, it would be 'It's Complicated'. This was my headspace every single day for many years.

I needed a good slap across the face.

Here I was, proud as ever that we had spearheaded a fast-rising fashion brand and yet, I purposely lowered the volume of that voice in my head because I felt guilty. I felt as though I owed the local fashion industry my life, and that I couldn't flourish on my own creative thoughts. I turned up the volume of the hurtful words said about me and downplayed my own achievements because I cared so much about being liked. The more books I read about this, the more I realized that this is a classic woman trait—we downplay ourselves, we care too much what people think, and we feel guilty about our success.

Le sigh

It took me a long time to realize that I *had* given my all. It was never part of the deal that I personally had to promote all the products under FashionValet, but I did. I wore local brands every single day, not just so they'd sell, but because I genuinely wanted to shout to the world about them. I photographed my outfits wearing them every single day even on busy streets, risking my life to get a good shot of their clothes. While influencers charge for postings like these, I did it all for free to lift up our local fashion industry. I paused every meal so I could flat lay my lunch with local brands' products; my entire closet is filled with local brands that I proudly bought myself . . . from a platform *I* created to showcase local brands. My love for local brands was (and is) genuine and no one could say I hadn't given my all.

But it was my time now to be given a chance to grow my own local brands. My chance was now to channel my own ideas and passion into building brands, which I could never do before because none of the brands before this was actually ours. The thrill I get from creating and coming up with collections and campaigns that can impact people—oh man, there's nothing like it. I enjoy it, and I shouldn't have to feel bad about that.

After I made peace with that, the guilt I had for creating dUCk changed to another feeling that also starts with g—gratitude. I cannot imagine where we would be now if Fadza and I didn't make the decision to start dUCk. I think back to the sleepless nights I had the day before dUCk launched, nervous to receive the response from people. I thought about the doubts I had about launching my own brand, and I thank God that He nudged me to do so. Because dUCk has not only been subsidizing to keep FashionValet afloat, but it has touched so many hearts and made a difference in women's lives. And I never want to clip its wings any more.

This was unfortunately the dilemma that we were in by creating two business models in one business. What happens when one significantly outgrows the other? But the smaller one involves the livelihoods of many entrepreneurs. For years, I tried to do good for both sides, but the journey eventually led me to a crossroad. That's the thing about entrepreneurship—you can plan and plan, but the journey will never be clear-cut. It's up to the entrepreneurs then, to make the best of it— that's why when investors invest, they invest in the *entrepreneurs* first, not the business first. The business might change along the way, but the spirit of the entrepreneurs is what will keep it afloat.

And just like that, suddenly, Fadza and I were about to make the biggest decision in our entrepreneurship journey.

Chapter 10

Business Pivot

Growing up, every family meal would be a philosophical lecture about life from my dad. Life is about this, about that, with some deep quotes here and there. Worse, he'd quiz my sister and me after to see if we listened.

'So, what were the 5Fs of Happiness that I just told you?'

My sister and I would look at each other, giving each other the you-can-answer-first look.

(It's Family, Friends, Faith, Fitness and Finance btw—there, a snippet from Uncle Yusof's School of Life Philosophy.)

I never knew how much his nuggets of wisdom have stuck with me, and now I couldn't be more grateful for them. I don't know if he quoted them from the books he loves to read or made his own, but it didn't matter to me. His words had been engraved in our brains such that every time I am unsure about something, I think of my dad and his words. They mean a lot to me.

One thing that I remember is him always telling us, 'Life is from B to D. From Birth to Death. In between, there is C and C stands for

Choices. Because life is a series of our choices, and we have to strive to make the right ones.'

Deep.

But he was right. Life *is* all about choices. And whatever choices we make, we have to weigh the pros and cons. There is no manual, no one to tell us which is the right or wrong choice. You have to take risks—choose and commit, no matter how scary the unknown may seem.

Fadza and I were about to face the scariest decision as entrepreneurs. We couldn't turn a blind eye any more because soon, we had to make a choice.

Common Sense Isn't So Common

No one knew the FV–dUCk dilemma from the outside. Internal people *must* have at least sensed it, but no one said anything.

We essentially had two business models running at the same time. One was the platform business, where we carried hundreds of brands and earned a commission when things were sold. The other was the brand business where we created and grew our own. They were very different animals, and we were always losing focus as to which one to prioritize.

Fadza and I are part of the Endeavor network, and if you haven't heard of it, Endeavor is a global network of high-impact entrepreneurs. You have to get in via a selection process and mentorship sessions to see if you're going to be accepted into this exclusive network. It's pretty cool—they take mentorship seriously, and once you're in, the global network just opens for you and you have access to literally every entrepreneur who has made waves around the world. Because of Endeavor, I got to go for a leadership course at Stanford and for a fashion tour in New York to meet fashion companies (that's when I met DVF).

One of our mentoring sessions, I remember it vividly, involved the Endeavor Malaysia Chairman at the time. He's a super low-key person yet highly regarded as one of Malaysia's best business leaders, running a multi-billion dollar telco in Malaysia.

'You mean you want to sell other people's brands while selling your own brands?' he asked after reading our profiles.

'Yes,' Fadza and I answered him confidently.

'Which one will you be focusing on more?' he asked.

'Both,' we answered.

'You guys are dreaming and need to grow up,' he told us with brutal honesty.

And that brutal honesty was exactly what we needed. Till today, he is our go-to mentor for everything and has become someone very dear to us. The brutal truth works wonders when you're making a mistake, when you're being deluded or when you're being plain stupid.

The numbers were very clear and were indicative of everything.

Let me share a little secret.

On FashionValet, the third-party platform business eventually contributed about 5 per cent to the entire revenue and was unprofitable—also most of the contribution here was of our outright buys, not consignment. Which means the business carrying local brands was not just unscalable, it was also extremely unprofitable. The remaining 95 per cent of FashionValet's money was coming from the sales from our own house brands that *were* profitable, mostly dUCk. We were investing so much money into both business models, but was this the right thing to do? Were we being smart entrepreneurs? The platform business was bleeding us into the reds, and the house brands business was making up for the losses of running the platform for third-party brands.

Fact is fact—our platform was losing money and was mostly being subsidized by dUCk's profits. For every piece of third-party brand we sold, the commission that we were getting did not cover all the costs of operations, marketing, payment and shipping, especially international shipping. In fact, this is true for most platforms and marketplaces you see out there—they're unprofitable. But that's fine for them because the business model they're after is a completely different one; one of hypergrowth and burning marketing dollars to gain market share hoping to be profitable *later* into the future. Where they will end up, we will have to wait and see, because one day, the profits will have to come from somewhere.

At the end of the day, a good business has to make money. It's as simple as that.

But common sense isn't so common if you are in too deep. The platform's unprofitability and unscalability were realities that were tough for Fadza and I to accept. *There must be a way*, we thought. This was the business that we built from scratch, our little baby! But if we kept on going, we would drive ourselves into bankruptcy. All the signs were telling us—our financial numbers, our competitors' unprofitability, the fact that we couldn't expand overseas with a website of local brands, and the rise of brands opening their *own* channels after FashionValet.

It was hard to scale, it was hard to get the local brands' loyalty, it was bleeding us dry. If this was a business case study I was reading about, I'd be like, 'Uhhh hello, shut it down, please?'

What are we still fighting for here?

Everyone already knew it.

But no one wanted to say it.

The reality was that the platform had to go.

The Endless 'Maybe's

I've read enough entrepreneurship books to know that it seems very obvious on paper—to cut the FashionValet platform. But none of those books tells you how hard it would be to actually *face* that reality head on. None of those books tell you *how* to know if you're making the right decision, or *when* you're supposed to let go, or *how* to handle the repercussions, or *what* to tell your customers and the brands who have grown with you. It was a tough period for Fadza and me, and together with our management, we had multiple offsites to see if we could save FashionValet the platform.

The endless 'Maybe's that we discussed:

- Maybe we need to get more brands for even *more* variety.
- Maybe we need to look at getting international brands instead.
- Maybe we need to *increase* consignment rate to make more money.
- Maybe we need to *decrease* consignment rate to be competitive.

- Maybe we need to do a full marketplace model to save our operations cost.
- Maybe we need to cut marketing budget even more to save cost.
- Maybe we need to do more collaborations with influencers.
- Maybe we need to invest in the local brands.
- Maybe we need to acquire the local brands.
- Maybe we need to hire more experienced people who have run platforms before.
- Maybe we need to hire different kinds of people since all other platforms are actually unprofitable.
- Maybe we need to assess if *we* were the problem, not the business model.
- Maybe we need to build more house brands to cover the losses of the platform.
- Maybe we should have a Local Brands Award to motivate the designers and brands to sell more with us.
- Maybe we should open more stores all over the country.
- Maybe we should look for more funding.
- Maybe we should work with banks to finance the local designers and brands' productions.
- Maybe we should work with other bodies to finance the local designers and brands' productions since the banks told us to fly kite.
- Maybe we should finance the local designers and brands' productions.
- Maybe we need to merge with Zalora.
- Maybe we need to merge with Lazada.
- Maybe we need to merge with Shopee.
- Maybe we need coffee.

We knew that all of the above required further funding and amplifying a business model that was essentially broken already and had no product–market fit globally.

Eventually, it came down to . . . Maybe we just have to accept the fact that FashionValet, the local brands platform, has run its course and it's time to evolve to the next phase to become the FashionValet *Group*?

Everyone kept quiet. The mood was sombre. We knew it in our guts, and we knew it from the numbers that it was the right thing to do. Yet, it felt extremely heavy to take a step towards it.

Show Me the Signs

In life, we will be faced with a lot of highs and lows, and a few crucial crossroads that will determine our future. You can talk to as many people as you want and write down all the pieces of advice that can fill up an entire notebook. But at the end of the day, the decision is yours to make and only *you* can rip that band-aid. And this is true for all aspects of our lives—career change, relationship change, health change, *any* change. No one can rip off the band-aid for you.

I had known this FashionValet reality for a while and in hindsight, it should have been earlier, but my competitive nature got the better of me.

Come on, Vivy, you're not a quitter! Come on, Vivy, you have to make it work, can you imagine the public embarrassment?

But how can I make something that's loss-making, work?

I don't know, but you're Vivy, you can surely think of something!

I was desperate to make it work and turn the platform profitable, so much so that I was ignoring this huge goldmine that was in the very room—the growth of house brands that was clearly being sidelined because of the need to focus on making FashionValet, the platform, work. That's why I no longer agree with the phrase 'Never give up' because it can blind you at times, when you *should* give up on something.

A turning point for me was reading this one book.

You'd think it would have been a business book that would have helped me in my career, but no, it was the unlikeliest—it was a spiritual book.

If you know me, you'd know that I'm a book nerd. I read a lot, and I even did monthly book reviews on my YouTube channel until I realized four kids really do take over your life. I'm mostly a sucker for biographies and business books, but I came across a series of books by Mizi Wahid, an Islamic scholar from Singapore. I admit the only reason I bought them is because of the hype—my friends were telling me about these books so I thought okay, this could be good for my book review. Plus, the cover is all minimalist and chic, nice to flat-lay. . . . #mebeingme

Little did I know this book would help catalyse the turning point in my career.

One fine afternoon, I turned the hardcover of *The Art of Letting God* by Mizi Wahid, and started reading. It's a pretty thin book so I breezed through it, nodding along as I read because so many things written were so true. It was basically about letting God in your life and trusting in Him when things happen or do not happen for you. Then one part made me pause.

On page 86, the book said, 'In order not to get lost and frustrated in life, we need to pay more attention to our intuition and gut feel. Every day more than a billion people ask God to "guide them to the straight path". But when He guides, many still choose to go the other way. Stop being a know-it-all. Stay humble, and connect with The Source.'

I looked up and started thinking about FashionValet *immediately*.

Typical, isn't it? When we read something, we immediately apply it to areas of our lives. This time, my mind connected that paragraph to what I was going through right now.

The words hit.

But when He guides, many still choose to go the other way.

Wow.

What was the point of me praying to God every day to help me on to the right path, help me make the right decisions, help me see things clearer . . . when He already *has* and I've just sat on the signs? And then prayed for even *more* signs.

If I could imagine God having a conversation with me, it would be:

Me: Please God, what do I do with my business right now? Show me the signs.

God: *shows numbers and graphs.*

Me: Please God, show me the signs.

God: *shows brands setting up own websites and not giving
   us stock.*
Me: Please God, show me the signs.
God: Sigh.

It's like I'd been knocked into seeing the real picture so many times,
but I was still closing one eye stubbornly. I'm sure many of you have
had this experience at some point in life. Maybe in your love life? Want
to leave a guy who is clearly not good for you and you know it, but
you close one eye. You know you're not supposed to be drinking that
sugared drink, but you close one eye. You know you're not supposed
to smoke, but you pretend to not see the gory photos on the pack.
Humans are creatures of habit, and it's never comfortable to change.

I remembered my Dad's 5Fs—one of them was Faith. I do believe that
it's so important to have faith in your life. To believe in God. Everyone's
spiritual journey is different, and we all have different bonds with God that
are unique to us. The way my husband 'talks' to God is very formal and
proper, which he is comfortable with. The way *I* like to 'talk' to God is very
personal—I blab on and on about my worries and troubles; sometimes I
wonder if God ever wants to hang up on me. But He never does. And I
know that because I'm always enveloped with this feeling of peace and
love that I can't describe, every time I 'talk' to God in my prayers.

Being an entrepreneur is extremely lonely, and you are often pushed
to the unknown without a GPS telling you, 'Now turn right.' Or left.
It's hard. And I truly believe that the only way this entrepreneurship
journey has kept me sane is because of my faith. I believe that He shields
me from what's not good for me, and He pushes me towards what is.

So when I read this line, I felt a deep realization that God has been
showing me signs me all along.

And just like that, suddenly, I knew what I had to do.

Suddenly, I felt really brave.

A Choice Was Made

Okay time to make that big C.

Time to make a choice.

I honestly can't remember how and when the conversation with Fadza happened, because the two of us had talked about this dilemma several times already. I don't think it was one moment, but several discussions that made us confident we were making the right decision.

Within that time, Fadza and I bantered and threw each other difficult questions about the future, and about ourselves, too. It got really personal, and that's why I absolutely love working with my husband. Your co-founder needs to be someone you can talk to, spar with, argue with, laugh with, have an all-nighter with—all of the above, and it's so rare to find one person who checks all these boxes. I usually don't advocate spouses working together because it is very risky (mind you, if FashionValet Group fails, *both* Fadza and I would be out of jobs with no backup).

I've always maintained in all my interviews that Fadza and I chose each other as co-founders because 1) we enjoy and respect each other's company and 2) we complement each other's strengths and weaknesses. Many times, people choose their co-founders based on convenience (husband, best friend, sister, etc.) but really, you need to make sure they have something to contribute to the business—even better if it's something that you lack, so you can complete each other because no one person can be good at everything. Fadza is operational and calm, I am creative and, well, not calm. Fadza is a man of few words, I am a woman of words, sentences and paragraphs. Fadza loves finance and operations, I love product and marketing. Fadza studied aeronautical engineering (whatever that is), I read law. Fadza loves museums, I love shopping malls. You get the point. But as opposite as we are, we come back together at the end of the day aligned with the same ambitions and the same values. And that's what's kept our relationship strong, be it in marriage or business.

It was important that Fadza and I aligned first, before anyone else. After that, it was time to talk to other people since this was a huge business pivot. We sought out advice from people we trusted. We consulted mentors and the global Endeavor network, we spoke to our shareholders, we spoke to other entrepreneurs—we were never shy to ask people for advice. A lot of these conversations shed new light on

FashionValet, and it was great because external people come in with unbiased and unemotional opinions. Most times, we feel like a decision is so difficult to make but others see it as so obvious and so simple that it helps knock some sense into us. Each of them had a different thing to say, but ultimately, it all led to the same outcome—it's time for FashionValet *the platform* to go.

To make any choice with confidence, do the work, ask God for guidance and trust in Him.

In Malay, there's a three-step guide we've been taught, which is exactly the above—*usaha, doa, tawakal,* which means hard work, prayers and surrendering to God.

We'd done our research, we'd consulted many people; we were now ready to rip off the band-aid. The emotions will always linger, but to be honest, when you're confident you're doing the right thing and you've done all the work to back it up, you feel strong. And suddenly, a wave of excitement comes knocking because you get to chart your journey all over again. The possibilities were endless, and the door was now wide open to whatever opportunities we wanted to reach. And this time, Fadza and I were taking that leap with ten years of experience. Twenty years, if you combine both of ours. With eyes wide open and carrying confidence and courage that can only come after living through many mistakes ourselves.

We were ready.

We were not afraid any more.

Let's pivot the business.

A choice was made—to shut down our much-loved platform and focus on growing our brands individually instead.

With fireworks in the background, wind blowing through our hair and a superhero soundtrack playing in the air, we marched forward.

Get to Work

You can stop that dreamy moment once you tell the team.

'What do we tell our customers?'

'So wait, where will our in-house brands sell?'

'What do we tell the brands?'

'Can I tell our buyers they can stop begging for stock from brands now?'

'We have some tech enhancements for the current FV website. Does this mean we stop work?'

'There will be no retrenchment, right?'

'What will happen to the FV stores?'

'What do we tell the media?'

POP.

POP.

POP.

The sound of the team popping my imaginary yellow balloons that read 'BRIGHT FUTURE'.

It wasn't going to be so easy. To shut down the platform, so many things had to be considered.

Where do we even begin?

We wanted to shut down the platform business and grow the individual brands' business, but they were intertwined. Our in-house brands were selling *exclusively* via the FashionValet platform. They *needed* the platform.

This was when we got our heads together to chart out the plan. It made me realize that making the decision was probably the easiest thing to do, but handling the consequences of that decision *after*, was complex. We had to consider every detail and every timeline. Thoroughly. Every stakeholder, every employee, every brand, every department, every customer, everybody who was touched by FashionValet before, needed to be considered.

It took months of planning. We had a committee that met weekly. Everyone gave their full commitment to this new direction.

The new goal was clear.

We no longer wanted to be a local brands platform.

We now had a new goal.

We wanted to become the largest modest fashion group of companies, growing local brands of our own and making them global.

Brands that we could control, brands that could scale, brands that could be leaders in the modest fashion industry. A niche, yes, but a niche owned by the second-largest religion in the world, a niche worth USD 277 billion in 2021. I'm all right with that.

We all saw the potential, and more importantly, we all knew we could be the global leader in this if we focused. We had the know-hows of growing brands, we had in-house tech with our own systems and IPs, we had both online and offline knowledge, we knew production very well and we had global connections.

Now that we didn't have to worry about a platform business, we could focus on just this.

With clarity comes power.

Now it was time to power through and press the accelerator.

Everyone in management believed in this new vision and wanted to be part of history of getting FV Group to that global stage. In the conversations to follow, it was really refreshing to hear our team use words like 'evolve', 'next phase' and 'next era', instead of 'closing' or 'shutting down' or 'failed'. No one in the company really saw the FashionValet platform closing as a failure, which was different from how I had felt in the beginning. It's mind-blowing to see how emotional attachment to something can really cloud your judgement and you see things how you've psyched yourself to see them. While others saw it as a natural progression of the company to the next phase, I was beating myself up for not being able to make it survive. Whether they realized it or not, my team helped me so much in staying strong.

CEO's office led this project and every week, there was a progress meeting to get updates from each department. It was like a machine.

Tech team was preparing for the new look for the FashionValet website, sans platform, and working on the websites and apps for our in-house brands (finally, a dUCk app, guys!). My Creatives team was busy ramping up product and marketing to strengthen each in-house brand to go out into the big bad world on its own. Operations team was redesigning the warehouse to devise the most efficient process for the brand operations. Logistics team was busy arranging stock returns to all third-party brands. Strategy team was preparing plans for each in-house brand to scale, locally and internationally. Retail team was busy managing the closure of FashionValet stores and planning the retail expansion plans for our in-house brands. Finance team was shifting budgets while ensuring that our cash flow was A-okay. The buying team was preparing to communicate to all brands that FashionValet was transitioning, and we would no longer be carrying brands on our platform. Commercial team was busy clearing stock and making the final sales on the FashionValet platform. People team was busy planning communications to the rest of the company and planning the new organizational structure.

Mind you, we were doing all this while juggling our day-to-day tasks at work.

Mind you also, we were doing all this during lockdowns from our own homes #thankyoucovid.

It was hard. But I felt such gusto and spirit from the team, especially during this time, everyone working together seamlessly to make this work not just for us but for the rest of the company. A strong team that gives you their full support honestly makes all the difference. Our support system within the company was unquestionable.

I mean, not only were we going through this tough business transition, but being in fashion, we were also part of one of the industries badly hit during COVID-19, because let's face it—who needed new clothes or scarves or shoes? Everyone was at home! Our stores were forced to close. We had zero offline income. ZERO.

But because of brand love, amazing customers, the focus on ecommerce and quick product pivots, somehow we powered through and even grew in revenue. It was unbelievable.

The thing that kept me up at night during this and during Covid was literally—can I pay salaries at the end of this month? I can bet you that was every entrepreneur's worry, on top of worrying about them and their families getting COVID-19. Our employees' incomes meant their families' food on the table, and that responsibility is Fadza's and mine. To make sure we steer the ship in the right direction. *We cannot disappoint them*, we told ourselves, and this was the fuel that kept our fire alive, to keep us going during the pandemic, one of the toughest periods for us.

That's when I knew we humans are capable of so much more than we know. Fadza and I had to oversee the entire transition of every single department in the company. At the same time, we were in lockdown with our children at home. There was nowhere to run from them #wetried. Going through a business pivot, making the biggest decision of our entrepreneurship life, having back-to-back meetings to strategize in between fighting over the wi-fi connection because the kids had online classes at the same time, and running around the house chasing our naked children because they refused to shower . . . was a lot.

But weirdly enough, our kids made the business pivot a lot easier to handle. Having kids meant that your stress level could be pushed to the highest limits—sleep deprivation, noise pollution, long to-do lists, ad hoc requests—and they still ain't got nothing on parents, fathers and mothers alike. I have been trained to think of creative strategies even with Cocomelon blasting in my ear. I have been trained to type fast with one hand while breastfeeding. I have been trained to have back-to-back meetings even while carrying a human the size of a watermelon in my tummy. Parenthood makes us stronger and difficult things don't seem so difficult any more. Because come what may, I gotta solve it now because I need to sort out dinner for my kids after this.

Parenthood is amazing for building resilience.

I clearly loved it so much that I popped four kids out of me.

Highly recommended. #haha

So yes, we went through a lot emotionally and physically during this phase, both professionally and personally. But at the end of the day, we survived and thrived.

Like Frida Kahlo said, 'At the end of the day, we can endure much more than we think we can.'

That is a great quote to remember for entrepreneurs, when our days seem dark.

Celebrating a Decade of FV

On the morning of 16 November 2020, Fadza and I wore all white and drove to the office. We had our party hats on. It was a special day. FashionValet was turning ten that day.

It had been ten years since that one fateful traffic jam. It had been ten years since we made the website go live. It had been ten years since I had my head in my hands with all sorts of nerves. It had been ten years since I roamed the streets of the city begging clothing stores for their manager's name card. It had been ten years since friendships were formed with local brands and colleagues. It had been ten years of countless ups and downs; even this book isn't enough to do justice to each beautiful memory.

I dreamt of a huge one-decade birthday party, at a hall somewhere with a band and lucky draws and games. Covid took that dream away, and FashionValet's tenth birthday party was not one that I had dreamt about. In the office that day, there were only about twenty of us, and the rest of the team dialled in because of the social-distancing rules. But we always knew how to make the best of every situation, and we all had smiles on our faces.

Everyone wore white, even those from home, and some had party hats and cakes, ready to celebrate from their own homes. The excitement for our beloved company was buzzing, and no social distancing could take that away from our hearts. We sang, we cut cake, we watched a presentation of our memory lane set up by the team. Fadza gave a speech, and I read a poem I wrote for FashionValet's tenth birthday.

I had tears in my eyes writing it, because 1) I was kicking myself for procrastinating while trying to write a poem at 1 a.m. on the birthday itself, and 2) it was bittersweet reminiscing the good old days all the while knowing that I was about to close that chapter.

Sharing with you what I wrote:

Dear FV

It truly feels like just yesterday,
We said let's make a website.
Little did we know that till today,
We would no longer sleep at night.

Growing you is a rollercoaster ride,
A ride that is filled with ups and downs.
Our first baby, we really tried,
To make you shine above other crowns.

The first of its kind in your country,
That's a lot of burden to carry.
Now that you're ten, let's have a party,
To reminisce, to smile and be merry.

You've given your all to build other brands,
For the next decade, it's time for yours.
All the lives that touched your hands,
You'll carry in your heart forever, of course.

I write this the night before your tenth birthday,
Tears fill my eyes, I had to take five.
For your success and happiness, every day I pray,
Dear FV, you've given us life.

We've made friends, we've made families,
At this very place, we grew every day.
You've showered us with lots of memories,
Some good, some bad, but come what may.

The next decade, we'll march in strong,
To the global stage, there's much to do.
We'll fight our best to do you no wrong,
For dear FV, we'll always believe in you.

Some people cried. #justsayin

What made it even more special was the fact that among those twenty people in the office, one of them was Asma'.

She was no longer working at FashionValet, but our friendship had remained as strong as it had ever been. The three of us (Ajjrina, Asma' and I) had always been there, through all of our ups and downs, and whatever hurt me at work hurt them too. They didn't need to work at FashionValet to feel the love for it. FashionValet's success was their success too; they wanted to see it bloom just as much as I did. You need best friends like these who pull you through every single time, best friends who drop everything to be with you and cry with you and then smack you out of it. That was us—AVA.

(To my other friends, don't worry I love you guys too, okay? *nervous laughter*)

When we went down memory lane in the presentation, I looked back at Asma' (in white too—very respectful of dress codes, I appreciate it), and we exchanged smiles. A bittersweet one. She knew about the pivot. She knew about the platform coming to an end. It made a mark in her heart, too. Especially because she was there from the start, carrying her FashionValet name-card that said 'Head Buyer' even though we only had one buyer (her), running in heels all over Kuala Lumpur, Jakarta and Bangkok to sign on brands that opened their doors to her, sitting on the floor counting their stock, staying till the wee hours to fold clothes with Fadza and me. It must have been as hard for her as it was for me because she poured as much heart into it as I did. We talked and talked about how big FashionValet was going to be, how it was going to change the world.

It was the three of us ten years ago—Fadza, Asma' and I.

And on that day, it was the three of us again, reunited to celebrate the mutual love and respect we have for our baby, FashionValet.

We'd come full circle after a decade.

I wiped my tears because our baby was not going away; it was evolving to enter its next phase in life. It may not have been what we thought it would grow into, but that's life—full of surprises and twists and turns. That's why to every card you're dealt in life, give your full heart and soul. Do not do things half-heartedly. Because only then will you live a life of no regrets. FV platform had to sunset, but I have absolutely no regrets knowing that I've given it my all.

Over the years, there was a lot of sadness FV had to endure, getting rejections for funding, getting rejections from brands, getting rejections from opportunities overseas. But it all makes sense now. All those rejections needed to happen for us to realize that we had the wrong business model. All those rejections needed to happen for us to create dUCk and other in-house brands. All those rejections needed to happen for us to thrive *later*. All those tears I cried when things didn't work out for the platform—little did I know that God was protecting me from digging a deeper hole.

We may not realize that most of the time, rejection is God's protection.

Chapter 11

The New FashionValet

I wish we had a crystal ball because had I known it was going to be this good, I would have done it sooner.

The business pivot (or as I prefer to call it, business evolution) was going really well. The decision to focus on growing our own brands felt like heavy dark clouds had moved away and bright sunny days were coming.

We still had to run the platform for a while more to avoid abrupt reactions from customers and brands. We had many focus groups, and customers needed time to adjust, and this worked well for us because the tech team needed to work on the brands' own websites and apps—it was like starting from scratch all over again. We had the option of continuing to sell our house brands under the FashionValet platform only, but decided that the brands need to be able to scale on their own channels. To keep them on one platform only was convenient for the group, but not for the brands in the long run.

From the outside, it probably wasn't clear to people because there were literally no new brands or stock on FashionValet—everything was just from our house brands, dUCk being the biggest one fueling the group. There were even talks that 'FashionValet is not doing well any more' here and there, but we didn't mind because we knew it was the complete opposite, internally. Our finances were finally in the black, we were not burning money on dead stock, we could control our own supply chain, and sales was even growing well with only our house brands.

That November, Fadza pointed out randomly, 'Do you realize that this time every year, you would be super stressed because you were begging designers to sign on their Eid collection on FV?'

I was so busy planning our house brands' growth that I completely forgot about that.

Every end of year prior to this, I would have sleepless nights because I would be visiting every designer in Malaysia to make sure they carried their Eid collection on FashionValet. Eid is the peak period, and designers knew that platforms would be knocking on their doors. It was always FashionValet and Zalora going head to head, and of course, Zalora having the bigger reach, it was always a challenge for us to win. Designers would keep us both waiting as they weighed their options, and it would leave the team and me waiting in agony. It was absolutely horrible having the fate of your business in someone else's hands, and I certainly don't want to be in that position again.

'Oh my god, you're right. Those nights I couldn't sleep because they were going to "get back to me" or because "Zalora offered to buy double"—ahhhh I don't miss those moments,' I replied.

It was nice that with the new direction, I could gladly tell brands to go to other marketplaces—a stark difference from when I was constantly fighting for them to stay with FashionValet. Felt like a whole weight had been lifted from my shoulders—there was no more FOMO if brands joined other platforms, and to be honest, it was nice to instead just remain friends with them. Just friends, no expectation of wanting their stock or anything. We can finally have lunch together without talking about how FashionValet was going to market their collection. I truly embraced JOMO instead—joy of missing out. At the end of the day, these are my peers, and I'll always be rooting for their success. I loved that local brands were thriving now and that FashionValet acted as a stepping stone to their debut into the world. We took a chance on local brands by providing the platform for them to thrive, and now that they have, it was also time for us to bow out.

Of course, there were some brands who didn't like this new direction but that was a bullet I had to bite. People won't like change, especially if the change does not benefit them. Some saw us as competition now, which I guess is fair. But honestly, I couldn't worry about that—I gave the ten years my all, and now, I too was evolving to the next phase.

Moving Forward and Prioritizing

Focus.

Such a simple two-syllable word, yet so difficult to achieve.

I'm a restless person, so I'm used to having ten things on my to-do list, and still feeling like I'm not doing enough. Weekends with me are a pain, because when there is so much free time, I want to do a gazillion things, and I end up feeling frustrated that I can't add more things. If an average person has three things on their list that day, I have ten. And even then, I feel like I'm not doing enough. It's really bad because you end up feeling overwhelmed, dissatisfied and never having peace of mind.

Entrepreneurs are full of ideas and so impatient that we want to do it all. *Simultaneously.* We think we're an octopus with many hands for some reason. We're always wanting to push boundaries and tell ourselves, 'I can, I can' even when we're burnt out, because we've committed to so many different projects. Looking back, I wish there were more times I said *no* than *yes.* I took on too many projects, thinking that all these were opportunities that might not come again, so I better grab them now. At one point, I was managing seven house brands and was stretched to the bone, yet I still felt like I wanted to add more brands.

I feel like the past two years have really been growth years for me, both personally and professionally. COVID-19 has given us the gift of not only more Netflix and Korean dramas (CLOY, anyone?), but also the opportunity for a lot of self-reflection. As much as it sucked, it really helped us review our paths. On a personal level, Fadza and I started to do a lot more charity work (during the pandemic, we raised via the FV Group more than RM 5 million to help hospitals and people who have lost their incomes), and we also thought a lot about how we were going to improve ourselves as spouses and parents. Professionally, we thought a lot about how we needed to evolve as leaders and what we have to do for the growth of the group to become a *global* brand.

One of the things we listed down was 'simplify the strategies'. This was our opportunity to have a blank canvas, and this time, with the learnings we've matured with. We redefined the FashionValet vision, mission and values, and we decided to narrow down even further to keep only two brands in the group for now—dUCk and a new brand we created, LILIT. Both played in the modest fashion niche.

That's it. Nothing else.

No platform talk, no new brands talk, no 'but this one has potential too . . .' talk. It was crystal clear, and weirdly enough for octopus me, I was actually excited about this simplicity. I remembered that Steve Jobs came into Apple to lead for the second time and the first thing he did was cut hundreds of projects—focusing on only a few instead.

dUCk and LILIT. already had traction both locally and internationally, and that's without much marketing. dUCk, being one of the few premium modest fashion and lifestyle brands in the world, deserved our attention to really scale now. While dUCk operated in the premium space, we created LILIT. in 2019 to fill the gap in the more affordable essentials of modest fashion. LILIT. was relatively new, but growing so rapidly that it had the potential to become the leading modest fashion brand globally—a one-stop centre for affordable and size-inclusive modest fashion. We weren't worried about competition, because when it comes to growing brands, so many things are brand-specific that cannot be replicated. It's very different from platform businesses, where it's harder to find that unique differentiator or customer loyalty, unless you keep throwing discounts that eat up your margin. The best advice I've ever got from people on competition is don't focus on competitors, focus on your customers instead.

With dUCk and LILIT. able to fill gaps in the modest fashion industry, we had to put our entire focus here. We were good at growing brands, now we needed to put these two brands on steroids and really scale them good. A fire lit up in me, for all the right reasons. The excitement of growing something great in the world that could actually fill real gaps in the market—what took us so long?!

From thereon, there was so much to talk about. Reallocating budgets, resetting brand directions, reviewing product assortments, planning retail expansion, restructuring teams and processes, building up the middle management, hiring new expertise to scale, hiring an international team, beefing up technology features, doing market research and customer focus groups—it was THRILLING. The atmosphere was fast and aggressive within the group, and I loved it so much. We tried to do this with FashionValet before, but now I understand why we never got there—because it was the wrong business model for us to scale. This time, it felt like we were finally getting it and the healthy financials helped validate our new direction.

We got busy.

In fact, we got busy personally, too.

We had another baby during Covid. #oops

See?

Octopus.

(Fadza made me promise this was the last baby. We shall see . . .)

Restructuring the Company

With this new direction, we also had to think about a new structure within the company. Learning from other fashion companies around the world, we found that everyone had a different way of operating internally and that gave us comfort that there was no cookie-cutter structure. You just have to do what you think is best for your company and just commit to it. Set a time to review it later and tweak as you go.

Through Endeavor, we got hold of a senior at Inditex Group, the group that owns Zara. It was one of the most valuable hours in my life that I spent speaking to her, learning about how the biggest fashion beast in the world runs their structure and operations. Reading about it is great, but actually *speaking* to them about it was a whole different experience.

This lady joined Inditex when they were making millions of dollars in sales, and helped grow the Group to *billions* of dollars in sales. She immediately became my girl boss idol. I mean, how many of us can actually say that on our resume? At Inditex, the brands were free to operate independently and creatively, but the commercial departments are shared, e.g., logistics, finance, HR, tech teams. The brands even compete with one another, oftentimes making the same products, which was something Inditex had no problems with. I learnt a lot about this—to not be too protective of the brands, let them compete with each other and uncover the best in themselves.

I asked her, 'How do you make sure you are being fair to both brands? Sometimes I feel like the mom in the company.'

'First of all, you shouldn't be the mom of the brands. It's not your job to be fair to the brands; ensuring they can meet their fullest potential—that's the team's job. You should most definitely focus on the bigger brand because that's the survival of the entire group.'

Marry me, Inditex lady.

That talk helped us put things into perspective, and we got to work.

We agreed that a specific team to focus on each brand was best, but with our size, resources and talent, it was smarter for us to still have a semi-centralized structure. Fadza and I decided that only the brand teams should be brand-specific, while the support teams would be brand agnostic. We divided the company into three groups—a dUCk team, a LILIT. team and a centralized team. The brand teams would be focused on the respective brand only and take care of the creative functions (product and marketing). The centralized team would cover all the support functions for the Group—operations, supply chain, retail, tech, people and finance. The brand teams report to me, and the centralized teams report to Fadza.

This was the best way for us instead of trying to hire two ecommerce managers for both brands, two retail directors, two supply chain managers, two of everything. Everything was still connected, and we put structures in place to ensure that each brand was given the time and attention by the centralized group, while balancing their own creativities. It was important for us to have specific brand teams because if the same people took care of both brands, product and marketing would eventually look the same. dUCk and LILIT. are two distinct brands with different brand positionings and different target markets. They cannot be run by the same team.

After a few months, we saw results. The brands grew multiples in revenue, the teams were more focused, the products were selling well, and marketing was more targeted. We ramped up retail stores for both dUCk and LILIT. in locations that suited each brand—dUCk in more premium locations while LILIT. had more choices for locations. We launched dUCk and LILIT.'s own websites and apps, and slowly converted FashionValet's traffic to the brands' channels. We knew this was going to be a long transition, because customers had been used to shopping at the FashionValet platform for a decade already. Inviting them to browse a new location after a decade was going to take some time, so we did not close down the FashionValet site immediately. Instead, we did things like exclusive website and app launches and discounts on the brands' side, to pull the traffic slowly and give existing customers the time and space to get used to the new look. With digital marketing and all sorts of product launches and activities on social media, both brands garnered new customers on their own, so it was a positive indication that they were going to be fine going out independently.

That's not to say all was peachy in the New FashionValet realm.

Transition Period and Morale

We were still in the transition, and in any transition phase, it's always messy and takes a lot of patience. Structures were changing, new ways of working were being introduced, and this would undoubtedly rock the boat a little bit. As humans, we like stability so when change happens, it worries us.

I wish transitions could be easier, but they don't happen overnight. We tried to do our best to keep the team morale high. We were always transparent in every townhall, and the managers had regular 1:1s with team, but there were times we failed. People were burnt out with the pressure and changes, some were double-hatting on projects that involved pre- and post-transition work (heck, I was quadruple-hatting at one point!), and they admitted to not having the patience or fire any more.

This was all happening on top of the pandemic, so everyone was working from home and feeling the stress of isolation. We did a lot of mental health talks and team activities online, but it was obviously not the same as being together physically. People team worked their butts off to plan team-bonding activities every week such as treasure hunts, chit-chat sessions, quizzes, contests, and I'll forever be proud of that passion for keeping the team together. But alas, the chaos from the transition was inevitable, and understandably, not everybody was enjoying the ride.

We lost some team members through not just resignations, but to competitors too. It gave us some comfort that this was a global phenomenon—CNN called this period The Great Resignation Wave. During COVID, businesses were all desperate to go online so there was a lot of poaching happening within FashionValet since we were known as an ecommerce company (70 per cent of our sales come from our online channel). Every other week, we'd get told that so-and-so was offered a higher salary or a better package by a competitor—this was obviously annoying, but at the end of the day, if someone wants to leave, you should not hold them back. One foot was out the door already.

This was something Fadza and I had to learn for many years—I used to get so emotional when people wanted to resign. I took it hard, kicking myself, thinking that I must have been a bad leader and this and that. I know this is something that strikes a lot of entrepreneurs' hearts too, based on the messages I get from some of you, so let me tell you that it's completely normal. You must always be ready to let people go if they want to go and remind yourself that they're not your friends, they don't owe you any form of loyalty, so it is not fair for you to expect that of them. In fact, thank them and give them a good send-off because they helped contribute to your growth journey.

Be good to your team. Love them, show them respect, lead them with heart. But every leader needs to protect themselves, so remember this:

1. Don't worry about resignations. You will be okay, and the company will be able to move on.

2. Don't get too attached to your colleagues. Be kind to everyone, but always have it in the back of your mind that they might not be with you forever.

3. Protect access to your company plans. This is something that Apple, especially, does a lot—Steve Jobs was so paranoid about company plan leakages.

Everybody talks about mental health of employees, but the mental health of an entrepreneur is equally crucial—you crumble, the entire ship crumbles with you. The amount of stress an entrepreneur carries is something no one will understand until they experience it. You must be strong mentally in order to hold the fort for all your team members. So do whatever it takes to seek help, be it talking to other entrepreneurs or counselling sessions or de-stressing with hobbies. For me, talking to my loved ones really helps me de-stress. For Fadza, it's working out.

What is your way of de-stressing? You have to find it.

Culture Change

As much as I miss my colleagues who left, I also saw this as a silver lining. When the business strategy changes or when you're at different points of the business, you will need a different set of skills—the same people who did the job five years ago may not be the right people to do the job. At FV, especially in the early years, it was a family culture—everyone ate together, everyone helped here and there, everyone felt close to one another. They were really good times, but honestly, not sustainable.

As you grow to hundreds of people (and I can't imagine how it'll be like when we reach thousands and tens of thousands one day), all that had to change. Key performance indicators (KPI) had to be set, low performers had to be put on performance improvement plans (PIP), and Fadza and I could no longer be on personal levels with everyone in the company. But because it was deeply rooted in FV, even worse because Fadza and I have humanized the company so much, it was very difficult to change this culture. People said we had changed, that FashionValet was not like before any more, that it didn't feel like family any more.

But it shouldn't.

I read so many company culture books to help me understand how to handle this change. The best ones were *The Hard Things About Hard Things* by Ben Horowitz and *Powerful* by Patty McCord. *Powerful* talked about the Netflix culture, and I was so inspired by it because of the spirit that Netflix trickles down throughout the company. Of course, I have no idea what it's really like to work there (I'm sure it's not for everyone) but seeing how they've grown and scaled globally, my googly eyes are just watching with admiration. They're famous for their culture deck that has been viewed five million times on the web, and I especially love the way they give their team a lot of freedom with accountability.

On page 24 of their 125-page (I know right . . .) culture deck, Netflix rejected the notion of companies being like families. 'We're a team, not a family. We're like a pro sports team, not a kid's recreational team. Netflix leaders hire, develop and cut smartly so we have stars in every position.'

They treated every phase of their company differently. Just like when you are on a children's sports team, the skills needed are different. When you grow to join a high school team, you need a different set of skills. When you grow to join a national team, you need a different set of skills, too. So just like the business, the skills needed are going to be different at different stages of the business.

We weren't a startup any more. Now it was time to scale, and we needed to hire people who could do just that. Fadza and I keep reviewing *ourselves*, too, to see if we have what it takes. When we know we have no idea how to do this or that, or we face new territories, we hire the right people to do the job because we weren't going to be the best at it. We only know what we know, and we have to make space for people who can actually move the needle for us with their experience and skills.

In 2020 and 2021, we brought in a total of 200 new team members, all recruited with the new business direction in mind, so almost all were perfect fits for the new FashionValet. Almost half the workforce was new, and with that wave will come a new culture. Processes and practices that even Fadza and I weren't used to, but we had to accept and adapt to. Fadza and I were excited about this change because we could focus more on strategy and the overall vision of the group. Fadza especially loved that we were more data-driven and tech-driven now, and the possibilities of global growth were endless now that a lot of things were being professionalized and automated.

We hired an experienced Head of People to transform the culture at FV and together, we improved on a lot of things. One that I will share is our FV values, which we fondly named 'The Red Carpet' to commemorate the beginnings of FV's first office—remember? That hideous but nostalgic red carpet that was on discount. The idea of calling it that is to show that this is the path that any FV Group employee walks on.

We have six values:

1) *Act Like an Owner:* Make your own decisions and your own mistakes.
2) *Be A Spongebob:* Learning is lifelong, and we regularly conduct learning sessions that we call Spongebob sessions so we can all soak in knowledge like a sponge.
3) *Customer Is Bae:* A mindset of 'customer first' in anything we do.
4) *Teamwork Makes the Dream Work:* Goes without saying!
5) *Dare to be Different:* Always strive to be the trendsetter and unafraid to experiment.
6) *Bite on Humble Pie:* To have humility and always think about doing good to the community.

There is no point if these values are pasted in our office lobby and everyone just walks past them without fully embracing them. We use them daily, in our conversations, in our performance reviews, in our company activities. We even made Whatsapp stickers out of these values with cute illustrations that we use in our daily conversations—highly recommended. I know the culture will evolve, and everyone will adapt eventually, but it's up to the management to make sure the leaders first live and breathe these values and lead by example. And that starts with the founders—Fadza and I.

Leaders in Progress

'What is your leadership style?' someone in the crowd raised her hand to ask.

Fadza and I were on a panel, recently, to talk about the FV Group with budding entrepreneurs. We had just finished passionately speaking about the beginning, the challenges, the pivot, basically everything about the business. But this question forced us to reflect on *ourselves* as leaders.

It was a tough question because it was personal.

I remember I couldn't answer it well because I had not reflected on that. Everything is a rollercoaster in entrepreneurship; you don't always have the time to stop and think about these things.

I knew later why I couldn't answer it well.

Because my leadership was and is constantly evolving. I was in that funny, awkward phase of change, and I hadn't fully embraced it. I was still going through it.

Change is scary for anyone.

There was a case study about cigarettes: smokers were told they were going to die if they didn't stop smoking. And a huge percentage kept on smoking. So you can see from this that people would rather *die* than make a change in their lives.

I'm not a smoker, but to some extent, I understand how hard change can be.

With this bigger team, renewed focus and new leaders around, Fadza and I had to change too. We had to unlearn and relearn so many things because this was a new phase for us, too. Fadza answered it well when he said, 'We were used to managing people, but we now had to learn how to manage experienced managers.'

We had a lot of those in the team now, each coming in with a wealth of experience. Of course, we were so excited about that, eager to see new changes and breathe new life into the new FV Group. Some worked out, some didn't. It is never a guarantee that when you bring in someone experienced, it will make the company better. Sometimes there's no culture fit, sometimes the existing team doesn't get along with the new manager, sometimes the values clash. It was frustrating whenever it didn't work out, because you can't possibly know everything from one hour-long interviews. A fellow entrepreneur Bryan Loo (founder of Tealive) gave me some valuable advice when he, too, was finding leaders for his team: hire them on contract first, so there's a test period and it's fair on both sides to review whether to continue the employment or to part ways. Now, for any senior positions in the company, we also get them to go out for a meal with some teammates to see if the vibes are vibing. #tryingtosoundmoreGenZ

It's better to take your time hiring than to go through the pain of getting the wrong person in, who could potentially bring down others' morale, and then having that difficult conversation three months later, when probation ends, and then having to fix the morale *again*. That is *if* the existing team hasn't already left the company. I've experienced hiring the wrong fits for the company and it's painful—they come in with experiences that are old school, sometimes the key people under them leave. Once even an entire department left and Fadza and I had to step in. At the end, these wrong fits will eventually leave the company, and with that, also leave a big mess for the founders to clean up.

When it does work out though, it's like hitting the jackpot. We've had a few of those examples, and it really does lift the burden from the founders' shoulders when effective managers manage their team well, both in terms of results and culture. Tough task! That's why these managers are rare. Good at thinking both details and strategy, good at managing upwards and downwards, having both hard and soft skills with values aligned with yours *and* a generally nice person to hang out with? That's harder than finding a husband, guys!

Fadza and I then had to learn how to manage our company in a different way. We needed to give these leaders the spotlight with their team, so that they could lead effectively. We needed to butt out and give the new leaders some space. The worst thing is having your bosses in the same meetings or group chats when you're trying to find your footing with a new team. Slowly, Fadza and I left group chats and stopped attending meetings, instead replacing them with high-level, one-on-one meetings and quarterly business performance reviews.

It felt foreign, I have to admit. It was weird not knowing everything in the company, not knowing the teammates at the executive level, not knowing what the teams are working on. We weren't even sure if our messages and values were being trickled down healthily. We still have a hawk-eye view of the company's performance—at FV Group, we have a dashboard available to every team member, and this is used daily to check real-time sales from all channels, bestsellers, sell-through rates, inventory levels, etc. So I know at any second which store is doing the best, which promo doesn't work, which product needs restock . . . all the business stuff was at my fingertips. But the dashboard cannot tell me if there are smiles at the office, or who is having lunch alone and whether I should check in . . . you know, the human stuff that I naturally care about.

I think the change was weird for the existing team, too, especially those who have been with us for years. Fadza and I used to be hands-on leaders who would pack orders with them or set up railings with them or come up with marketing campaigns with them. I would go through every single product sample and approve them before they got produced. Nothing would get done without mine or Fadza's approval, which obviously was no longer sustainable at our size. But that was the norm before, so this change affected the existing team as well. There were so many instances when the team would message us directly whenever there was a decision to be made or a dispute to be solved. We had to resist the temptation of making that decision or solving that problem, because by doing so, we would be undermining these new leaders.

On top of that, I had to hold back on some things that were more personal, too.

My loved ones know that I like to put smiles on people's faces, I like to make them happy. I think of the people I like wherever I go. Even when I travel and see some cute souvenir, I'd think, 'Oh, so-and-so would love this!' If I see something related to cats, I'd think of a couple of people in the office who I know love cats, especially my own assistant, Ida. If I see unique post-it notes, I'd think of my colleague Rus, who was obsessed with post-it notes. If I knew someone in the company had just given birth, I'd rush to the hospital to visit them with flowers and balloons. If I was at one of our stores, I'd give the team at the store some pocket money for dinner. If there was a birthday, and I found out about it, I'd send the person a cake. I love people, and to me, who better to be kind to than your loved ones, including your colleagues? Soon, even that became a problem because it invited favouritism issues.

'If you send this person a cake, you have to send everyone a cake, Vivy,' my HR team warned me. Of course, that wasn't possible with almost 500 people in the company. I'd be sending a cake to someone every day of the year!

Even my friend asked me then, 'If you follow your staff on Instagram, don't you have to follow *all* your staff because some might feel left out?' as I was commenting a 'haha' on one of the Instagram accounts that I followed, not realizing I should then comment 'haha' on the other colleagues' Instagram accounts too. That's a lot of 'haha's, guys.

How would I feel if I saw my boss commenting on my peer's Instagram and not mine? How would I feel if I knew my boss sent my peer a birthday cake and not me?

I came across a comedy show from one of my favourite comedians, Fakkah Fuzz. He was coming to Kuala Lumpur, so I knew I wanted to get tickets for my friends and me. Then I thought, 'Hmm, the team has been working so hard lately and COVID's got everyone's morale down, so it'll be nice to get tickets for them, too'. So I did. We all had a great time that night.

A few days later, 'Vivy, I know you wanted to do a nice thing. But now the international teams are asking why there's nothing like that for them. They didn't explicitly say it, but I know that's what they're thinking. If we want to do a nice gesture, we have to do it for all our teams in other countries, too.'

Oh crap.

All these things that I never had to think about when we were a smaller company, were a problem now. All these habits that I had cultivated that came from a good place, were now becoming a bad thing. I had to slowly shake them off, and no matter how badly I wanted to send that person a birthday cake because it was just my nature to make them happy, I had to stop myself from digging a hole for myself and my company. I had to *stop* being nice *to* be nice. Ironic, isn't it?

This, and many other instances, were things I had to learn in order to evolve from a leader of a startup to a future leader of a global company. It used to be so natural to reply to an email or Whatsapp message instantly. It used to be so natural to see a problem and solve it immediately. It used to be so natural to pull up a chair and just have lunch with a colleague. It used to be so natural to literally know everything happening in the company and to be friends with everyone.

From Startup to Scaleup

The moment Fadza and I started changing to evolve, we saw a lot of the older colleagues leaving. Not all at once, but it happened one by one. They were honest with me, saying that the company has changed, and it was not like it was when we started. I gave them a big hug and said I would forever be grateful to have had all those early years with them. Whatever they said, I accepted and respected. Because it was true. It was not the old FV any more.

Everyone had to realize that we were transitioning from being a startup to now being a scaleup. The company needed Fadza and me to be on the strategy level now and let other leaders lead. If not, why hire them? Fadza and I needed to spend our time making sure the company grew exponentially in the next decade, and a lot of this time would be spent thinking about scaling and networking, especially overseas.

We couldn't be checking each sales promo any more, or checking each metal buckle on handbag samples; we had to trust the team to do that and let them go on their own journey to discover themselves as leaders. There will be things Fadza and I don't agree with or things we want to fix, but we have to balance it with wanting to respect the leaders' own leadership style or allowing them to make their own mistakes along the way. It wasn't a 'Fadza and Vivy' company any more, it was a company full of leaders, each one playing their part in steering the ship in the right direction together.

Even today, I am constantly learning, and my leadership style will continue to evolve. I used to be a hands-on leader; now I have to learn to commit to being a strategic leader. Leaders have to adjust their leadership style to adapt to what the company needs of them at that point in time. Right now, we are spending our time charting out our growth, so that's where I need to focus. But no matter what leader I am at any point, I will always be proud to lead with heart. I may not be able to send everyone a cake, but I'll always be me. I still want to be kind to people, to smile at my colleagues, to say thank you, and to work hard and smart, to ensure our team and their families' livelihoods can be multiplied. Apart from the commercial goals of wanting to build a global fashion group, a personal goal of mine and Fadza's is to make sure our team can be financially secured—there are a lot of things we want to implement for our team and their families, which hopefully you'll get to read about in a book about our second decade.

A favourite interview question is always, 'What does it take to be a good leader?'

whips out a long list of traits

There will never be one answer to this. You'll need a combination of so many things—determination, passion, energy, foresight, resilience, etc.

But one trait that stands out for me is the ability to adapt. An entrepreneurship journey isn't a straight road; it's full of winding roads, crossroads, highways and freaking roundabouts that you'll have to go through. Many times, you'll find yourselves having to switch gears, sometimes reverse, sometimes change the tyres, sometimes change GPS locations, sometimes even change passengers, in order to survive. If there's anything that the pandemic has taught us, it is that businesses need to be able to adapt. If they stay the same, they will die. A leader is to the business what a driver is to the car, so they have to be able to drive the business according to whatever situation or climate he is in. Adaptability is a skill because it involves changing—and if I hadn't made it clear, people hate change.

If I had to choose another trait of a leader, it would be good mental strength.

When I read Bob Iger's book about his leadership at Disney, I was in awe of what he went through during the opening of Disneyland Shanghai. He found out about the death of a boy in Disneyland Florida, which broke him, but he had to continue with back-to-back interviews and came back to the room and cried and apologized to the boy's parents. And then back again to meetings and more PR commitments, where he had to continue smiling. I cannot imagine the torture and how mentally exhausting this must have been for him.

But it wasn't any different for me. Of course, his was on another magnitude, but the conclusion was the same—that every entrepreneur needs to be mentally strong. Every entrepreneur needs to be able to control their emotions and have the ability to reset several times during the day. Because one minute, you can get bad news, the next minute you have to chair a meeting with twenty people. One minute, you find out your star employee has resigned, and the next minute, you have to make a presentation. One minute, you find out you lost a deal, and the next minute, you have to go for a media interview to talk about how amazing your company is. One minute, you find out your child is sick, and the next minute, you have to get on a plane for a work trip because ten meetings had already been set up.

It takes a lot of mental grit to be able to live like this day in and day out, and this is probably a *normal* day in every entrepreneur's life . . . for the rest of their life. Because the issues don't stop the bigger and more successful you are—in fact, they increase because the stakes are higher and you have more stakeholders.

I've had my mental strength tested many times in this decade. I would consider myself pretty strong mentally, but even the strongest among us can crumble. There were many instances that made me sad that I will never forget. Despite going through them, I would go about my day normally cheering on the team as usual and smiling at appearances. But no one knew that, at times, I was crushed by the biggest heartbreaks of my personal career.

Chapter 12

The Heartbreaks

The Price of 'Privilege'

I was scrolling through Instagram one day and came across a quote by Elon Musk. It said, 'Working 16 hours a day, 7 days a week, 52 weeks in a year and people still call me lucky.'

I stopped scrolling because that quote stuck with me. How many times have we heard people scoffing at people's achievements saying things like, 'He probably had connections' or 'He just got lucky' and more to invalidate their achievements? I hear it among netizens, I hear it at work, I hear it among my loved ones, heck, I even hear it in my own head sometimes, before I tell myself off. Why do we do this? Is it bitterness? Is it envy? Of course we're only human, but we have to get to a point where we can be happy for others' achievements, instead of downplaying them.

In the decade of my career, I've had my fair share of naysayers who would always invalidate whatever little success I had.

She already had followers so it doesn't count.

She has connections so it doesn't count.

She has easy money so it doesn't count.

She comes from a good background so it doesn't count.

All these above . . . are true, and I'm so grateful for them.

But that doesn't mean I don't work hard for the things I have achieved. My followers? They were built from years of me writing on my blog. Every. Single. Day. These same fingers typing this book are the same fingers that have been writing on that blog for more than a decade. I didn't write to get famous, I just wrote from the heart because it was my passion. I didn't care if two people (Hi Mom and Dad!) read it, or two million people read it. I wasn't writing to build an audience, and ironically, that is exactly *how* I built my audience.

My connections? They were built, not inherited. Again, *over years* of putting myself out there, joining public events and conferences. I'd be that girl queueing to ask questions at talks, and that girl who goes up to strangers at events, thick-faced, blurting out, 'Hi, my name is Vivy. What's yours?' I wouldn't just talk to business leaders, but I would talk to the event organizers, to the videographers, to the writers, to the waiters. I am a people person, and after some practise, networking came naturally to me.

My money? Apart from my dad's RM 50,000 loan (which was not free—I gave him shares and paid him back), nothing else fell into my lap. Fadza and I googled every potential investor and just like everyone else, we had to *work* to pitch our business idea to them. It took months and multiple meetings, and we faced far more rejections than successes. You've read in the earlier chapters of how we fundraised for the business—anyone can do it if you have a business idea you feel strongly about. Heck, we went on a reality show in front of the nation to ask people for money—and I'm still privileged?

My background? I will always be proud of my parents for giving me a life they worked hard for, and I can only hope I can do the same for my own children. But they never spoiled me without teaching me values—of humility, of kindness, of hard work. My parents both gave me a life of lessons and opportunities, and I am everything that I am because of them. I put a lot of pressure on myself to keep smashing that ceiling, because I don't ever want to let my parents' sacrifices be in vain.

You can't change your past and where you come from, and unfortunately, that will be a label you will carry throughout your life. People will always look at me and think, 'Ah there's that privileged girl', even if any luxuries in my life now were bought with my own hard work.

It annoyed me in the beginning, but then I asked myself, 'Why does it matter?' Why does it matter if people think you're a privileged kid who doesn't do any work? Why does it matter if people think you didn't deserve to get funding? Why does it matter if people think you are just being handed things all the time?'

I stopped, as if I had an epiphany.

Oh my god.

It really *didn't* matter.

After a decade of being in this, you will naturally develop the ability to lower the volume of the negative toxic noise and turn up the volume of the positive music of life. Even if people say things about you, you start to realize that they're mostly just noise that is masking the unhappiness that they have within themselves. People who say things behind your back will always be *behind* you, so leave them there while you charge head on to achieve even greater things.

You have to move on.

No Longer the Underdog

I equipped myself with this over the years to prepare myself for all sorts of things. People couldn't shake me with the privileged thing any more, so they started other things—they called me a capitalist because I sold premium products with higher price tags, they called me *poyo* (can't seem to find the English word for this!) because I appeared to speak more English than Malay.

When I was seen as the bigger brand, I was no longer the underdog. People started painting the image of me as a bully to smaller brands and really tried hard to pin me as this. I was called a plagiarist because some of our products shared similarities with other brands. Never mind the fact that I had never heard of any of these brands. Never mind also if the design element was universal, and many brands already used it. Never mind also if the accusations were simply made on Twitter or Tiktok, without any validation or fact-checking. Never mind also the fact that people were copying *us* a lot—no one wanted to highlight that. I mean, a brand made shoes with two straps, which, by the way, were everywhere in the shops and malls. But when my team made shoes with two straps, it was headlines that we 'plagiarized'. We made slippers with criss-cross straps. Again, a very common design anywhere. But because we did it, we plagiarized somebody. These allegations became a pattern and because of that, some brands took advantage and used them to get netizens to throw more hate to us.

Once, we had a dUCk scarf collection for Malaysia Day, inspired by Malay desserts. Someone tweeted that I had plagiarized their designs because they had illustrated Malay desserts too. I had never even heard of this person or seen the designs in my life, and I'm *pretty* sure they were not the only one in the world who had illustrated desserts before. But they were so convinced that my team and I had plagiarized them—going on to say we caused mental health issues to them and it took several years to recover. If my jaw could drop to Level Basement Parking, it would. I couldn't believe this at all. The way they made themselves sound victimized was implausible because we'd never crossed paths in life before! But they had so much support from netizens, some even encouraging legal action against me. I was left speechless when my team told me about this because (a) I had never heard of them or seen their designs, (b) Malay desserts were not created by them (or us!), and (c) do I really need a (c)?!

In 2020, dUCk had a collection called the Artsy dUCk, which featured a print of paint splatters and doodles. We felt like it had a childlike free spirit to it, so we collaborated with an orphanage—for every scarf sold, an amount would be donated to the orphanage. The children were so excited, they even made cards for the dUCk team and customers to say thank you. For the photoshoot campaign, the creative agency we hired suggested an artist-theme concept with easels, canvas board, and lots of paint and brushes. 'Makes sense,' I thought, since the collection is literally called The Artsy dUCk. When the team released the photos on social media, someone lashed out, saying that we copied their photoshoot from years ago, putting our photos side by side. It was a universal concept—artist in a studio—but netizens rushed to their side, directing all sorts of hate towards dUCk and me. I knew the person, so I sent a private message saying we did not copy them and that I apologize if they thought we did, etc. The response was a crying emoji and a continuation of publicly throwing hate at us, soaking in the attention that they had garnered. The entire time, I had the children in the orphanage in mind, my heart bleeding for them. I cannot believe how people can turn something noble into something ugly, just because our photoshoot had the same theme as theirs.

What was tricky about this issue was that many years ago, her collection was sold on FashionValet, brought in by one of our buyers. Because of that, it was easy to assume I plagiarised it—but I didn't think it was fair to expect me to remember every single collection and campaign theme from 500 brands and make sure I don't come out with anything similar, even if it's a generic theme. People hung this over my head all the time—anything dUCk did, there would be some people who would purposely look to find if there was anything similar that launched before on FashionValet over the years.

At the start of 2021, LILIT. launched an instant scarf using magnets. The idea was convenience—just snap and go. It wasn't a unique solution; many brands had already used magnets in their products and no one could claim they owned magnets. The team experimented on the magnet placements, magnet types, and finally, the teaser photo was released to social media before the launch. The product hadn't even launched yet, but it became viral for the wrong reason. All because another local brand also used magnets in their scarves, and the founder decided to make a Tiktok video of themselves crying. Literally crying. In the video, they were sobbing really badly saying that 'a big brand' had copied them, and they were just trying to make an honest living to help their parents. Of course, the video went viral and garnered so much love, which in turn meant so much hate for LILIT. We had never heard of them or the brand prior to this, and magnets were not theirs to claim, and yet we were villified for doing something we didn't do. Again, it became news on social media, and mainstream media eventually picked it up.

It got to a point where people just wanted to rope in my brands (dUCk, especially) into their posts because they knew that would be clickbait in itself. The crying entrepreneur had their products sell out because of this and quickly issued a 'thank you and we will restock soon' message. You're umm . . . welcome.

Once, there was a plagiarism claim happening between two brands (not mine, finally) in the local fashion industry. That made news too, but the title that was used for the news article was 'Vivy Yusof 2.0?' I remember the moment I read that. I was celebrating my mom's birthday, cutting her birthday cake and smiling at how happily the day was going— and my face just changed and I quickly told my mom I had a stomach ache when she asked what was wrong. In the bathroom, I held back tears and just thought objectively about the legality of this article. I was pulled into this news that had absolutely nothing to do with me and was being labelled something that was untrue, just for that portal's clickbait. I felt so bullied and asked my lawyer if this was a defamation issue. Needless to say, the article was quickly taken down, but it had already been shared and screenshot by the public. As people carried on with their lives that day, I continued with my mother's birthday with a smile, but I knew I couldn't hide the sadness in my eyes from her.

Social media is extremely powerful. Whilst most of the time, this is to our advantage, times like these can put a damper on the journey. No public figure in this world, whether you're a celebrity or an entrepreneur or a politician, is exempt from this: the bigger you are, the more of a target you will become. The moment you get called out by even just *one* person, it goes viral because well, bad news makes news. And it really doesn't matter if it's true or false, because the truth people believe is what's popular at that time. Because of the anonymity social media grants, people can hide behind keyboards and dish out the most horrible comments—we've even found out some were competitors taking advantage to amplify the negative news, and some created multiple accounts just so it can seem like more people are joining the hate. But it's important to note that even with all these, there are many more people who can think more wisely and see that there really is no issue or connection or even logic to these claims—but they can't say anything publicly because they will become the next targets of the online attack. They instead send me or the brand accounts some words of love privately.

When we ask the 'friendlier' netizens why they feel strongly about the claims, they answer that they felt pressured by their friends and that they thought they were helping to uphold justice. When probed more, they said they actually didn't really know or understand the issue or the law, but they felt bad because it seemed like a bigger guy bullying the smaller guy. One said they rushed to attack us because one accuser was crying really badly and said he started his business because he wanted to give money to his parents. I empathized with that, but I also looked at my team of almost 500 people. Are they all not working hard to give money to their parents, too? I could never understand this thinking of 'big brands must be hated on'—big brands also consist of hardworking people who need to feed their families; in fact, even more of them. Big brands also have to work hard; in fact, that's probably why they *became* big, and now most likely will have to work *even* harder because the responsibility is bigger and the stakes are higher. There shouldn't be a big brand versus small brand debate. A big brand started as a small brand too. At the end of the day, we are all working to earn an honest living for our families, and we can all make it together. We are all in the same boat.

I've always loved supporting other entrepreneurs—heck, the whole FashionValet concept was literally that. Whilst that business model did not make commercial sense, you would have read in earlier chapters that I really enjoyed seeing the impact it made on new and smaller brands. In my position now, with dUCk and LILIT., we try to work together with other brands via collaborations, and there is a lot more we want to do to bring the whole industry up as we grow too, but of course, news like this doesn't make news. 'Vivy Yusof helps other brands' is not going to be an article you would click on more than

'Vivy Yusof bullies other brands', and unfortunately, that is just how humans are wired. Bad news always makes better news, and that is something any public figure will just have to accept.

Even today, I don't know the best way to handle this issue. People remind me that big brands anywhere in the world get plagiarism accusations all the time. I was always told not to fight back, to 'be the bigger person', to not make things worse and amplify a small thing into a big thing by talking about it on my platform or the brands' platforms. Well, it seems like by 'being the bigger person', we have gotten this unfounded label of a plagiarist on our foreheads when we never did any of those things. It seems like our silence in response to each of the claims has made it worse, because as they accumulate over time, they have become the 'truth' that people repeat over and over again. I was always told that silence is best. 'Don't worry, God knows,' people would tell me. So I stay patient, hoping that there will be a silver lining one day. I am yet to see it, so I sometimes doubt myself on this 'silence is best' strategy, and that is just the truth.

Counterfeit

I love visiting our stores, and one day, a customer walked into one of the dUCk stores, wearing our most popular design at the time—the Kuala Lumpur dUCk scarf. She smiled at me but I was frozen, shocked.

I managed a smile back, swallowing the shock. The store team looked at me and I looked at them.

We were shocked because this customer was wearing a turquoise version of the design . . . but we never made a turquoise colour!

We soon discovered there was a whole market out there that was selling fake versions of our products. There were syndicates behind this, and they were growing bigger and bigger. There are many types of dUCk counterfeits—some exact replicas of fake dUCk scarves using low-quality material, some completely new prints but using the dUCk logo—all designed to mislead customers into thinking they're getting a dUCk item. One father bought his daughter a fake dUCk thinking it was real, and the daughter tagged me on Instagram saying it was the happiest day of her life getting dUCk as a graduation present. I didn't know whether to smile or cry.

These factories never make themselves known, and whenever we try to investigate, we find dodgy things involved. I won't go into them but one can only imagine if products are sold that cheap, are the workers being treated well? Are they using child labour? Is corruption involved? If the products are already illegal, do you really think they would play by the law when it comes to staff welfare and general work ethics? That piece of scarf on your head that you think is harmless, was it a product of bad practices that you probably wouldn't want to support if you knew? Most people don't know this or think much about it; they're just happy they got a version with a lower price tag.

We are always on the prowl for people who produce and/or sell counterfeits, and it is undeniably a frustrating pursuit. Sellers get caught, pay the fine, and then set up again using another company name. Even if the police did a raid, they may confiscate all the items that day, but the sellers would sell again the next day because they know the police wouldn't be doing raids daily at the same spot. There was a case where thousands of fake dUCk counterfeits were being traded, and when we did a background check, the company belonged to an eighty-year-old woman. The woman doing this with her husband had put her grandmother as the director of the company, so if I went after her, I would have to drag her grandmother to court. They were sly to exclude their names from the company and put their grandmother as the proxy. Anything happens, only the grandmother would face the consequences. As angry as I was, my conscience could never allow me to pursue that case. My own grandmothers would come back from the dead to haunt me in my dreams if I did that. I let the case go. Being human meant more to me than being right. I may forget that couple as I go on with life, but God won't.

Most of these counterfeits are not produced here but brought into the country from outside. We tried to get in touch with the customs authority to curb this issue—shouldn't they stop the illegal counterfeits coming into the country? But to no avail. Once, I had an audience with powerful people in the country—they wanted to know more about local entrepreneurs and the problems we face. I thought it was such an honour to have this once-in-a-lifetime meeting and was touched that they really cared to hear from local entrepreneurs in the country. I shared with them our blockers, including the counterfeit issue and felt a glimmer of hope when they seemed to show deep concern about it. After all, I told them, it wasn't just dUCk facing it—many brands in the country had this problem. Unfortunately, until today, the problem persists.

You can hope other people will care and help, but at the end of the day, that is just a bonus. It's on us to settle our own problems, not someone else's. We cannot just sit and wait for even the government to help us, because it may or may not happen. We did things that we could— we registered all our trademarks, we filed patents for our innovations, we hired IP lawyers to take legal action against the people who sold the counterfeits. So much money was spent on protecting our signatures and designs, but it was a necessary investment to protect our brand. We also reached out to all major platforms in the country to help stop the selling of dUCk counterfeits on their platform. Most of them were cooperative because they too didn't want to be selling illegal products. Some sellers still manage to sell illegally after finding loopholes in the system because of clever copywriting or tagging, but the overall problem was reduced significantly for us because of the platforms' cooperation.

The greatest power of all, though, was the collective voice of ours and our customers'. Our customers were our best advocates—calling out the fakes and bringing them to our attention. dUCk educates customers about the counterfeit too, from time to time. I even did a factory tour to show the process of making dUCk products, showing viewers the level of care and quality checks we put products through before the product gets released to them. I also compared the authentic dUCk product versus the counterfeit one to educate people so they don't get conned by the misrepresentation. I drove home the fact that dUCk was only sold on our website and stores, so we could not guarantee the authenticity if customers bought it anywhere else. That video had over a million views, and we saw a rise in brand love and more awareness in helping to curb our counterfeits.

I know that this counterfeit issue will never go away. If it could, you wouldn't see fake Louis Vuitton and fake Chanels today—but they're still widely sold in broad daylight in any country you go. What's most important, though, is just to focus on things we can control—our own products, our own innovations and our own branding. There will always be people buying counterfeits, but that just means we are doing something right, that people want to be associated with our brand. Hopefully, one day, they will aspire to buy the real thing and stop buying the counterfeits.

A Double-edged Sword

I remember a few years ago, I was at the airport and a group of girls wanted a photo with me. Fadza was watching from a distance, waiting for me, and a guy came up to him: 'Bro, who's that girl and why are people taking photos with her?'

Just for fun, Fadza pretended he didn't know me and told the guy, 'I have no idea'.

I get that a lot, and I guess it's hard for people to bucket me into a group. I'm not an actress, I'm not a singer, I'm not a celebrity of any sort, so it's hard for people to figure out why I have almost two million followers on social media.

'She sells things. She's an entrepreneur,' people would explain to their friends, sometimes awkwardly in front of me.

'Selling things can get two million followers, eh?' they would reply, with me still standing there, cheeks redder than tomatoes.

I don't know either, guys. I started as a blogger writing my life journey on a computer screen, and then I became an entrepreneur . . . who sells things. I have never wanted to chased fame, and even today sometimes feel uncomfortable with the attention. But I'm grateful that I have so many followers who support me and help put food on my table. With just a post, I could reach millions of people to promote a product. With just an unboxing video, I could make a collection sell out. Alhamdulillah for the reach that I am able to garner.

But nothing comes without a price.

Social media is also a double-edged sword. The more followers you have, the sharper the sword becomes. Any mistake I make gets magnified multiple times over. Any customer complaint gets blown out of proportion. Any similarity with any brand at all in the world draws plagiarism allegations. Any wrong post gets me in hot water.

Which is what happened in 2020.

Major Social Media Backlash

At the start of the pandemic, things were uncertain everywhere around the world—lockdowns were being imposed, people were experiencing anxiety because of the uncertainty, businesses were not sure if they could pay salaries or rent. It was a surreal year for everyone.

Governments everywhere were trying to find ways to save their countries and help their people. At that time, Malaysia announced individual financial aid for the people. Soon, businesses and retailers started realizing they, too, needed some help. They had little to no sales because shops were forced to close during lockdown, but of course, they still had to pay salaries and rent. Most probably had only a one or two months' runway before they ran out of cash reserves and would have to close down. If they didn't get any help, small to medium enterprises especially would go bust, and this would mean the loss of jobs for over seven million people employed by SMEs in the country. It was no joke.

I was watching a Facebook Live that was shared in our entrepreneur group chats. They were discussing this issue and concluded that SMEs should be given some form of help to save them. I found the talk interesting, so I decided to amplify their voices by posting it on my social media. With my reach, hopefully more people could rally to give support to SMEs in order to help these businesses survive. I am an entrepreneur after all, I knew how scared business owners felt at that time, wondering whether or not they could pay salaries by the end of the month. It would be devastating to see businesses close down and so many people losing their income and their ability to put food on the table for their families. As an entrepreneur, I wanted to help by raising awareness, too.

I posted a three-minute clip from that Live on my IGTV on my Instagram account, with a short caption to encourage support for SMEs. The first hour went by with lots of positive comments agreeing with this, but it quickly went down south.

In the three-minute video I posted, there was a part that one of the panel speakers said that became a contentious topic in the comments section. He said, and I quote:

'Government servants are receiving guaranteed salaries, and the question is what financial loss did they sustain? Besides addition of one-off payment, why the extra payments? . . . To me, the government is helping those who are not contributing, you know, to the economy. They are receiving money. There is no other financial relief for SME employers other than certain financial credit relief package.'

People in the comments section turned on him saying that the receivers of the individual subsidies were not contributing to the economy. Anyone watching the video would know that he did not mean what he said—he was stuttering looking for the right words but alas, the words that came out were that. I don't know any of the panel speakers personally, but I gave him the benefit of the doubt that it just came out wrong, which happens sometimes in live sessions. The line was just three seconds out of the entire three-minute video, but someone called him out on it, and it was just going to be a matter of time before he would get trolled on social media.

'I should take down the video, right?' I asked Fadza.

Fadza scrolled through the comments. 'Yeah, I think you should.'

I tried to archive the post, but IGTV does not allow for archiving. The only option to take an IGTV down, at least in 2020, was to delete the entire post. So I proceeded to delete the post. The post was only up for two hours and then disappeared forever, along with the comment section. I wrote a post to apologize for causing any tension within groups and called it a night.

Little did I know that that would be the last peaceful sleep I'd have that year.

Deleting that IGTV post would later become a big mistake. I became the number one trending issue on Twitter in my entire country. For all the wrong reasons.

What followed after was unimaginable. People were talking about my post, and because it was deleted, there was no evidence to refer to so people *made up* their own conclusions. Suddenly, the conclusion of the entire issue was that *I* said the entire b40 community contributed nothing to the economy. Before I could even do or say anything, someone made a graphic banner with my face on it with the words, 'Why does the government help the b40/m40 community when they don't contribute anything to the economy—Vivy Yusof.'

What Just Happened?

I was mortified.

I did not say anything of that sort. I don't even think anything of that sort. It was crazy.

That banner was shared and reshared all over Twitter, Facebook, Instagram, you name it. It was forwarded in Whatsapp groups, even to my parents. My Whatsapp was buzzing with friends and media wanting to get in touch, and I got really worried. I've been slandered before on social media, but this time, it was on another level. It felt dangerously different. My stomach churned, I felt hot everywhere, and there was a huge lump in my throat. I felt my eyes fill up with water. I could feel tears coming. I felt alone, angry, scared—you name it. The retweet number kept going up every few seconds, and there was absolutely nothing I could do to stop this slander I was being subjected to. It was blatant fake news, and I was at the heart of it, and there was nothing I could do to stop it from spreading.

People grew angry after reading that banner, and who can blame them? If I read that someone said that, I'd be angry too, especially if I didn't have any context. People rode on the news, making their own spinoffs. I remember a Malaysian social media influencer posting about it saying he lost respect for me, and riling up more anger among Malaysians towards me. More influencers followed to take advantage of the situation and draw more attention to their accounts. Netizens were sending hate comments on my profile, telling me that I should die, that I was just a piece of shit, that they hoped someone would burn me alive. What reduced me to tears was when I read a comment saying they hope someone would take my kids and drown them in the ocean because they should not live through life with me as their mother. It was extreme and *way* out of line.

People smeared my name all over town, including the media, which amplified the news to the masses. Without any proof, any fact-checking, any reference to anything—just that one single navy-blue banner. That banner still haunts me today. There was no proof of me saying this one-liner—no video, no screenshot that anyone could ever produce because obviously I didn't say it. I felt so disappointed that people would believe things without even any proof, and even help to spread it around. All the world had was that banner that someone made of me, and they just believed it. I think about who this person is, who actually took the time to make that banner: does he or she not worry about the day of judgement?

It wasn't enough that I was getting hate on a national scale.

Suddenly, a petition happened.

I was the youngest member on the Board of Directors of Universiti Teknologi MARA (UiTM), the biggest public university in Malaysia. Because of this social media backlash, someone in the alumni started an online petition to remove me from the Board. The link was shared in so many Whatsapp groups, and people were encouraged to forward emails to their friends. Ironically, one email was sent to me, and when I clicked on the link to see, a prompt said, 'Thank you for signing the petition', which showed me that some configuration had been set that when someone clicks on the link, it automatically registered as a signature. So there you go, I signed my own petition. It was a really weird day.

Whether the petition was rigged or not didn't matter. The fact was that the petition went viral and pretty soon had garnered hundreds of thousands of signatures. The Board assured me that this was no grounds for removal because there was absolutely no proof, and it was blatant cyberbullying. But soon after, a letter was sent to my office by the Minister of Higher Education: she terminated my tenure without any reason and I was asked to leave the Board so I respectfully did so.

The level of hate and cyber bullying was so bad that I lost 3 kgs in two days, something I thought was scientifically impossible to do. My loved ones were affected, of course. My parents phoned me every few hours to check up on me, my husband was constantly supporting me, my best friends cried for me and my colleagues wanted to fight the netizens for me. They were so sad at how this had turned so wrong so fast, of course, because they knew the truth. But millions of Malaysians didn't.

I wanted to fight back. I wanted to release that video again to show that I didn't say such things. I wanted to reply to all those horrible comments. But I held back. Everything I did on social media that week had to be thought through, had to be vetted. I had to be super, extra careful. It dawned on me then that whatever I say, even one word wrong, could lead to a national catastrophe.

People concluded that I didn't want to help the b40 community when I was *literally* working with NGOs to donate and even raising money to help them through the pandemic. I got scared to even say anything. I did speak to some people, including PR firms who reached out to help me do damage control, and the general consensus was that the best way to handle this was to just keep quiet and let the issue die down.

But how do you sit back and watch the nation spread such lies about you? It hurt so bad. Here I had the chance to correct the narrative *and* the platform and reach to do so, and I didn't want to do it? That seemed crazy to me. I started my journey as a blogger so sharing my thoughts was what I did best! I was used to sharing aspects of my life and being my authentic self in front of everyone. Now I had to hold that girl back because the stakes were high—I could no longer be that young and carefree blogger who could write anything she wanted. I felt like I was being silenced from being the very person that I am inside, and I felt frustrated at that.

No! Stand up for yourself, Vivy! I told myself. *Who else will do it for you?*

My parents warned me against saying anything further. 'You will not win this, just let it go,' they said but I couldn't just sit there.

So I went against their advice and released a video to say that I didn't say those things, and I would investigate this the proper way. At the end, I apologized for causing the unnecessary drama and hoped that everyone could be kind to one another.

The next day, the headlines in the media were 'VIVY YUSOF APOLOGIZES.'

Another headline, 'VIVY YUSOF WILL TAKE LEGAL ACTION.'

What?!

That's it?

Where's the part that I denied saying those words?

On that video alone, I received 20,000 comments. There were a lot of encouraging comments from people backing me up, but they were all getting attacked by the haters. People were afraid to defend me publicly because they would get 'cancelled'. So they would send me support messages privately telling me that they're sorry this is happening to me and reminded me to be strong. It was bizarre that someone was told to shut up when she was literally trying to tell her side of the story.

My parents were right. I stood up for myself and somehow made it even worse. I realized it didn't matter if I was telling the truth or not. People didn't want the truth. People wanted the drama, they wanted to believe that you were wrong. They wanted to see tears and see people dragged through the mud, because . . . it was fun for them. It wasn't about justice. In light of the frustration and instability that the pandemic was giving everyone, they needed an outlet to channel their angry energy. Unfortunately, I became an outlet.

That issue was laid to rest and people moved on, but not without leaving multiple scars and wounds on my heart. From time to time, I think about how I could have handled the situation better, but I feel sad knowing that I was being slandered for something I didn't say or do, and then being told to 'go shut up and die' when I defended myself. This side of humanity can be so cruel, especially behind anonymous keyboards.

But *c'est la vie*.

But How Could You?

Getting hurt by strangers on social media sucks, but honestly getting hurt by people you trust unlocks a whole other level of pain.

At work, you're bound to create bonds with your colleagues. You'll feel a sense of closeness, and you might gravitate to some people more than others, especially if you have more projects with them. It's the same with entrepreneurs, too. You will trust them with many things— your vision, your hopes, your dreams, your strengths, your weaknesses, your happiness, your sadness. They will become your confidantes and best friends, because let's face it, you spend more time in the office than anywhere else.

Things will always be peachy during happy times, but as entrepreneurs, we must remember that our colleagues, unlike us, can leave at any time. They might ride the ups and downs with us, but some things may come to an end. For some, it may be a year; for others, maybe a decade or more. Every journey is different. But the reality is that they can move on to other things, and while I wrote earlier that I'm grateful for them, sometimes their departure can create a void in your heart for a while.

It especially hurts when they leave to go to a competitor brand. It happens often, of course, we hear people move from bank to bank, from agency to agency, brand to brand . . . it's so normal. But to a founder, it hits differently because you're more emotionally attached to the business than others. As much as you try to keep it professional, you can't help but . . . be human.

It's bizarre to see people who were once rooting for the company, and riding through each memory with you, suddenly switch to the other extreme when they join a competitor. Before they leave, your colleagues will always say, 'I'll always be rooting for you', but the moment they join a competitor, they start poaching your suppliers, your key staff, your plans, your partners. Because they have to now think in the best interest of their *new* workplace, even if it means stealing your people and your ideas.

These things happen, and it honestly hurts. I fail to understand the conscience of people who earn an honest living in one company, have that company be good to them, keep everything on good terms, etc., and the moment they step out of that company, do things like use their strategies or poach their staff. They know very well it might hurt that company, but suddenly, they don't care. I get that it's all professional, but at some point you've got to question, where do you draw the line between being professional and being human? Because you're in a workplace, all your good values as a human being exit the door? After 6 p.m., those values come back because you become a normal human being again?

And don't think just because they were the trusted ones, that they would be excluded from this. Sometimes the one closest to you, the one you trusted most, will be the one that will hurt you the most. Because they know everything *and* more about you and the company, they are even *more* wanted by your competitors. You might think, 'He'll never do that to me,' but you never really know when you're sleeping with the enemy. It happened to me once. I lost a key member *and* close friend to a competitor, and there were so many 'How could you?' moments that played in my mind and my heart. I didn't have to get angry, though, because people in the industry got angry *for* me. Word got around that my friend did this to me and people saw that friend differently. I didn't have to say anything. When money and power are on the table, people can turn on their loved ones and drop their promises and values in a heartbeat. So unless you can see the future, just like anything else in life, you should never trust anyone 100 per cent.

You can put so many things in place—limited access to information, NDAs, non-compete clauses, but humans being humans, things will always slip behind your back. Suddenly, you'll start seeing competitors copying you—whatever your collaboration, they will follow suit. Whatever your products, they will start launching them too. Whatever your unique selling points, they will start emulating them too. You can choose to take legal action against a former employee using your company information, of course, but you must always see if it's worth your time and money or not.

I learnt from my experience. At first it was hurtful and annoying, when the competitors started following in our footsteps. But after a while, I realized that it never hurt my position—my company was still thriving, and my team and I were still innovating constantly. I started to see that even customers could conclude for themselves that some brands are always copying us and making comments—and don't think customers are not smart, by the way! They totally know which people from dUCk went to other brands, especially our long-time loyal dUCkies.

Over time, I became less bothered about these things because nothing changed for the worse for us. If they keep following us, they will always be that—followers. Suddenly, my perspective changed. I realized that all I had to do was focus on my work and my team—that was it! We stopped looking left and right, and we just put our heads down to keep on innovating and keep on serving our customers. There was actually nothing to worry about when it came to competitors, because in the words of McDonalds' Chairman Ray Kroc, 'They can try to steal my plans but they can't read my mind'. Every company is unique because of the founder's vision in his or her mind. So if you think about it, every company is different, every brand is different, and we should not have to worry about competitors. They can steal your plans, but they can't steal you and your mind. Just like how you too can steal their plans, but you can't steal them and their minds. All the negative emotional stuff between competitors is merely a distraction, keeping all of us away from what we were supposed to mind—our own business!

There was a quote I saw on Instagram that made me chuckle because it was almost like a reminder of what I was feeling that one particular day: 'If you focus on you, you grow. If you focus on shit, shit grows'. So the lesson of the day, always focus on you. Don't allow yourself to get caught up in a loop of self-pity and worry about things that are not within your control. You can't control what your ex-employees do. You can't control what your ex-boyfriend does. You can't control what your friends do. You can't control what anyone else does—full stop. But you *can* control what *you* do. So focus your energy on things that matter—you and your company.

While my dad is the one pushing me to be driven and entrepreneurial, my mom grounds me to have the ideal balance. Her favourite advice to me that keeps me sane is this—what's meant for you will always be meant for you. That line alone has kept me sane whenever I've needed a little assurance in this journey. What's written for you will always be yours, and vice versa, if something doesn't happen for you, it wasn't meant for you. In Islam, there's a simple phrase in the Quran, 'kun faya kun' (36:82), which translates to English as 'be, and it is'. That phrase reminds me to never fear anything because if God wills it, it will happen no matter what. It's not your call, or your competitor's call— it's His. If He says 'be', it will be.

Focusing on the Good

It's very easy to focus on the bad stuff. One bad news can ruin your *entire* day. One hurtful comment can ruin the entire post. And that's the funny thing about us human beings—even when ten things are going right, we tend to focus all our energy thinking about the one or two things that are not.

Typical case scrolling through Instagram: Smiles at the nice comments. Sees one bad comment. Thinks about that one comment the whole day.

Isn't that such a waste of a day?

As entrepreneurs, there will be ups and downs daily. Some projects will fail, but you forget about the ten other projects that went right. Some people will betray you, but you forget about the other hundreds who didn't. Some people will try to bring you down, but you forget about the many other people who are pulling you up.

Same thing with life. We complain about our spouses sometimes, but we forget about the hundred things that they've done for us. We get mad at our kids sometimes (okay, most times), but we forget about the times they make us smile. We focus on what we don't have, but we forget about the many things that we *do* have.

With this simple shift in my perspective, I got to see the world in a whole other way. Through the lens of gratitude, of beauty, and of optimism. The energy changed, and instead of focusing my energy on the negative events of my life, I'm now constantly reminded of the amazing things that are around me. It has made me handle my stress a lot better, and things that used to bug me don't bug me as easily any more.

Whenever anything bad or negative happens now, I have that mindset of not letting them win over me. Being the competitive person that I am, that mindset really worked for me because I needed to win over myself. When negative thoughts enter, I tell myself not to let those haters win against me. When I feel angry over something, I tell myself 'don't let the devil win against you'. I control my thoughts, I control my actions—no one else should be able to dominate that.

Because even with all these things happening, the truth was that our business was thriving. We lost some people, but got better ones. We lost some followers, but gained new ones. We never lost hope and because of that we always came back better and stronger. We focused on what mattered and kept our eyes on the ball, and the company became so much healthier and stronger. Never once did I feel like giving up and throwing in the towel. No. Life goes on, business goes on, the show must always go on.

So whenever you face hardship privately, publicly, professionally, personally, I hope you will remember my favourite ayat in the Quran. In the words of God, 'Verily with hardship, there is ease' (94:5). He repeated that twice, by the way!

These episodes of heartbreaks did not break me permanently. I'm still here standing, and in fact, it's taught me that in whatever I do, I need to uphold my integrity. Don't fight with people, don't criticize people, don't backstab anybody. People can try to paint you as a bad person, but so long as you observe your ethics, there's nothing more that they can say.

Refrain from giving in to the temptation to do questionable things because people around you can also make their own judgements. They might smile at you, but inside, they don't trust you. Investors don't just invest in businesses; they invest in the people. If they hear that Fadza and I don't have integrity, and we backstab people to get ahead, I can bet you they won't put their money on us. Same with our friends and our employees. If they know their leaders are the type who will cheat and lie to get ahead, they know in their minds that those leaders can leave them dry at any time too.

Business is business, but we are all human beings, first and foremost. Not excluded from the day of judgement, not excluded from karma and not excluded from guilt and conscience.

Be an honourable person.

Win with integrity.

Chapter 13

Days Ahead

If I were to list down all the challenges of growing a company, this book would be many inches thick. There are the big issues, and there are also the everyday issues you have to think about—inventory holding, supply chain problems, cash flow planning, dead inventory, constant product innovation, hitting targets, people issues, etc.

And here are some reassuring words to all budding entrepreneurs, on the next page . . .

The problems will never stop.

Haha!

Okay, you still turned the page.

Good to know.

Awesome application of mental strength right there; pat yourself on the back.

Jokes aside, I wasn't joking. The problems will *not* stop. In fact, you will have more because the bigger you grow, the more complex your company will be. The more attention you get, the more haters will come. The more people you pay salaries to, the more families you'll be responsible for. An entrepreneur needs to accept that that is the life you will have. It won't be easy, but I promise you it won't be boring either.

I won't be very popular for saying this, but I truly believe an entrepreneur is *born*. It's not just about growing an idea, but all the other things that come with it that will require you to have that grit, that passion, that willingness to be thick-skinned, that mental strength to be ridiculed and rejected. This may not be everybody's cup of tea. This may not be the life you want for yourself, and that's okay. You just have to be honest with yourself—do these challenges excite you, or do they terrify you?

Starts with a Dream

A few years ago, Fadza and I passed by a street in Bangsar, an upscale neighborhood in Kuala Lumpur. I pointed to a corner of one of the malls there. The corner shop lot was lined by beautiful trees, facing the busy street with an outside entrance.

'One day, that will be a dUCk store.' I sighed as I pictured it in my head, leaning against the car window.

It will be a massive duplex store with lots to offer—maybe even a café in the front to give customers a complete experience. The coffee will have a dUCk logo on it, which people will take photos of. Products would decorate the store beautifully, encompassing the whole lifestyle of our customers from apparel to scarves to cosmetics—oh, maybe then we can have bags and a home and living categories, too. Could we have a food range as well to upsell at the café? Oh my god, we should have a salon! I pictured groups of girlfriends having fun in that private salon, their hijabs off and just having a damn good time together. All at this one dUCk store.

Fadza held my hand and smiled, always amused by my non-stop thoughts and dreams.

Today, as I write this particular page, was the launch day of dUCk's flagship store. At the very same location that I pointed out to Fadza years ago, in the story above.

I'm looking at a photo that Asma' sent me of the store that she took earlier—a photo of the store entrance, with a reflection of a rainbow curved across it. On top of those doors was written 'dUCk'. The store (yes, a duplex!) comes with a salon, a café, and with that little dUCk silhouette in coffee cups—all the things I dreamt of having. There was a line of people waiting to enter, excited for what I hoped would be their new hangout spot. That ray of light shining at the entrance made it a whole lot more special, reminding me of hope and dreams— among many others, that dream that I had a few years ago, which came true today.

Earlier today, I got dressed for the media event in conjunction with the store opening. It felt so surreal that my vision for this had come true. It took years, of course, but still. I manifested this, I dreamt for this, I worked at it and it came true. It always starts with a dream.

Back Down to Earth

This cloud-9 moment above lasted for a few hours.

After the store opening, it was back to meetings and work and Whatsapp messages to reply to.

There is a flurry of unread messages on my phone since I spent half the day at the media event mingling with guests. Apparently, there's a problem with delayed stock arrival of a very important upcoming launch, and we have to explore a virtual launch, which means all the stores won't get it on time. Then there are updates about dUCk app issues. Our Head of International needs confirmation on some things urgently. Also getting an update that two department heads are bickering with each other and can't seem to come to a solution. Inbox beeped—someone just resigned. Oh, man! Next email below that—Bloomingdale's Kuwait wants to stock dUCk! Oh wow, that's awesome. A new message came in. 'Vivy, have you had a look at the 11/11 campaign? Just wanted to hear your thoughts before I proceed.' Ah, I can't think about that now. There's a meeting happening in five minutes about LILIT.'s sales and cash flow projections, and Fadza and I need to confirm the numbers so the team can start executing.

I just opened my dream store, for God's sake.

Can I get five minutes to appreciate this moment?

Nope.

And that is the reality of being an entrepreneur, if you're crazy enough to want this. #haha

An entrepreneur's life is fast-paced, like tennis balls that are being thrown at you non-stop. Some balls are good news, some balls are bad. Either way, you have to acknowledge every one of them and not let them drop and accumulate, making you trip over them and land on your face.

I clicked on the Instagram app on my phone—hundreds of kind DMs from my followers congratulating the team and me on our latest flagship store and expressing their excitement to visit. Ah, what a delight to read.

One message said, 'How do you have it all put together so well? Everything seems to be going well in your life'. I looked at that message for a good few seconds and chuckled.

If only that follower could see me now.

I'm back from the media event, and my feet are red with blisters from the heels that I had to wear for six hours this morning, I have an ice pack on my back because of the back pain from my heels. I have heat patch stickers on both temples because I have a headache from pregnancy nausea. Oh, I'm pregnant as I write this, by the way, just days away from my due date . . . I have unread messages from my direct reportees that I have to address ASAP. I forgot to pick up Sarah from school today, and I also forgot to order lunch for Daniel and Mariam since I couldn't cook today. And I'm *pretty* sure I'm having mini contractions right this second. Oh and I also decided to write a whole book about this life, so I'm writing really fast, struggling to finish this book before I pop! I can't put my legs together any more when I sit, because the baby's head has engaged down there. So here I am, writing to you in the most unattractive state of me sitting with my legs spread out. Sorry if that's too visual for you, but if you've reached this chapter, I think we're pretty close already.

This, guys, is the life I chose.

The entrepreneur life.

More specifically, a very pregnant mompreneur life.

Is Entrepreneurship Hard?

You bet!

Is it fun, though?

Heck yeah!

A lot of people say entrepreneurs must be crazy to want to go through the pain of entrepreneurship. Re-reading the chapters of this book, even I think, 'Wow, that's a lot to deal with'. But it's pretty amazing to look back at the past decade and realize we survived all that, and we're still standing. Standing taller, even.

Through all of the sucky parts, there are so many thrills that come with my job. It is so easy for us human beings to focus on negativity, and in that process, we don't pay nearly enough attention to appreciate the positives. The tech team just rolled out their plans for so many features to build a truly omnichannel group of brands. My retail director just spoke to me about all the malls that are offering us lots and her plans for retail expansion, in and out of our country. My product team is updating me about some really cool innovations, including making scarves and clothes from fabrics out of waste coffee grounds and cut-down trees. My marketing team is gearing for a huge pop-up in the middle of the city centre, something no local brand has done before. The international growth team is making plans for expansion that I'm so excited about.

There are a lot of things going right, if we choose to see them.

As for me, I just finished an interview with the renowned *Business of Fashion*, speaking about the huge potential of modest fashion and being one of the few in the world selected as a thought leader for this piece is such an acknowledgement. In front of me, Fadza is preparing for our upcoming board meeting and the exciting plans for moving forward.

There's no looking back. Right now, we're just a speck in a sea of opportunities and growth. There's still so much work to be done and so much room for growth. It sure feels like Day One all over again, which is so exciting, except this time, we come with bruises and scars that remind us of lessons and wisdom we've collected in our first decade.

So you see, through it all, you have to pick what kind of person you want to be. Do you want to be the person who only sees the problems and then complains on social media? Or do you want to be the person who sees the potential and then bulldozes through, come what may? If you're the latter, I can't wait to read about *your* first decade, because I'll be rooting for you.

Closing My First Decade

There are many things I didn't achieve in my first decade. My hopes of being a billion-dollar company was not met, I had the wrong business model to scale, and I am not nearly where I want to be yet. But I realize now that this was what I had to go through to learn, to fix things, to get the team and systems ready, to get *myself* ready—as an entrepreneur, as a leader, as a partner.

Fast forward to today, and I couldn't be more grateful for the decade so far. Sure, I would have done some things differently. Sure, I wish we had pivoted into the new direction sooner. Sure, I wish we were bold enough to cut the cord much earlier when things did not work. But everyone's path has been determined, and this was mine. It took a decade for me to get to this point, but that decade taught me so many lessons to prepare me for the next one.

God is never late. Wherever you are, trust that that is where you are meant to be right now.

No one knows what the future holds, but I sure am excited to find out. I'm sure the next decade will be equally, if not more, challenging, but I know it will be just as fun and thrilling. We can always plan, but God decides. I don't know where my entrepreneurial journey will take me, but I trust wherever I'll be, I will have no regrets.

I'm happy to have crossed paths with you, and that I got to share the ups and downs of my first decade, in the hope that it will help you navigate yours. As you can see, this was not a success story—it was just an honest story from an entrepreneur who is still crawling through this journey full of crests and troughs. And this entrepreneur hopes that her stories can help other entrepreneurs going through similar things and let them know that they're not alone.

I'm entering the second decade now, but it wouldn't be right to do so without first thanking the first decade for all it has taught me. So thank you for the beautiful memories and hard lessons, my first decade. I will always carry them in my heart for the journey ahead.

And with that, I will march on with a smile, closing this chapter of my life—The First Decade.

Acknowledgements

I have birthed four children from my very body, and I can now conclude that writing a book is more difficult than that! What I thought could be a three-month (max!) project turned out to take much longer than planned, because completing a book takes discipline and patience—both values absent from my DNA.

It's a miracle that this book is in your hands, and I thank God first and foremost, because none of this could have happened without His blessings.

So many people have helped, too, and I hope you'll allow me the space here to thank them.

My amazing parents, Yusof and Aishah. Dad and Mom, nothing in here would have been possible if you both didn't meet and, you know. . . #eww. I owe everything to you both, and I can only hope I made you proud, despite the pain and heartache of raising this stubborn daughter of yours. I love you both so much, and I hope I can one day give you both the life you absolutely deserve. Nothing good happens without our parents' blessings, and I must be the luckiest girl to have always had you two as my pillars of strength. If people call me privileged, I would say the biggest privilege I have is the honour of being the daughter of the two most amazing parents who have hearts full of love and care for their children.

To Intan, my sister, thank you for always looking out for me and being my rock. Growing up, it was always just you and me keeping each other's secrets from Mom and Dad, and till today, I'm so grateful that we still have each other's backs. Although I hope you've come to terms with the fact that I will always be the favourite child.

My kids, Daniel, Mariam, Sarah, Idris (insert any more, if any, at time of reading . . .), you rascals have no idea how much you've completed my life. I've complained about each of you during my pregnancy and even more so during labour, but please know that Mommy loves you soooooooo much. I hope you'll read this book one day (in between your precious video games, of course) and know that dreams do come true if you work for them. I'll need you to work for yours so that you can take care of me when I'm old and buy me things I like.

To my in-laws, thank you for always rooting for me and helping me keep my kids alive while I had to write this book. Especially to my mother-in-law, Nasimah. Mak, I cannot imagine not having you in our lives. Thank you for always being there for Fadza and me, helping us with everything imaginable, from school pickups to home-cooked meals. Thank you also for letting me borrow your handbags—you may never see them again.

Ajjrina and Asma', you know it's lame when you're nearing your forties, and you have a name for your posse. But I'm all AVA, loud and proud. It's pretty crazy that not a day goes by that we don't write a gazillion texts to each other. Our husbands say we have no boundaries— if only they knew our plan to move in together when we're old and grey (with or without them). Thank you for EVERYTHING. Thank you for being on this journey with me, listening to my every sadness and happiness (and by every, I mean *every*), and cheering me on to never give up. People dream of true friendships like this, and you both are really lucky to have me.

Marissa, our six-year-old selves are clapping for this near three-decade friendship. Thank you for not just being there for me, but actually WITH me in FV through ten years of your life—I'm forever grateful to you . . . and your banana muffins.

To my ducks in high school until now, Tasha (who is still my colleague woot woot!), Sara, Sofia, Hanaa—I'm so lucky to grow up with amazing girlfriends and even though we are scattered in different countries now, distance never stops us from sending 320 WhatsApp messages everyday about the randomest things. This friendship will be forever, especially because you have too many old teenage photos of me.

A special shoutout must be given to my friend Sofia, because without you, I wouldn't even have a blog to begin with. My entire journey started because I was a blogger, and if it wasn't for you being annoying that day and forcing a blog on to me, I wouldn't be here today. Thank you for also making me Alex's godmother (okay fine, you didn't, but please consider).

Kim, my personal highlight with FV is when it brought me to you. We started as colleagues and it has blossomed into this clingy friendship. Thank you for being my shoulder to cry on for so many things, and I expect your shoulder to be stronger for the second decade, thank you.

Alia, you've always been my voice of reason for so many things. We've been through so much together, all the ups and downs at work and in life, and I hope we will always power through together come what may. Don't forget our dream of being roommates in London . . .

Stella, that first day in university witnessed a crazy fun friendship that I'm always grateful for. You were my first friend to have met Fadza and gave him a nod of approval—it was either him or that Jeremy guy . . . Thank you for always sending me boosts of motivation and always telling me I can reach for the stars, from university until now.

Ian, my childhood friend, thank you for still sticking by me through all these years and telling me how proud you are of this Malay friend of yours. I think it's really sweet that you try really hard to shop from dUCk even when there's really nothing for you. I'll make you a tie or something soon.

To the boys in my life—Afzal, Anand, Seth, Jason, Yusuf, Aiman, Normann—life would be so dull without you and your lame jokes in the groupchat—I won't admit it again but they keep me happy during the toughest days at work. You guys don't show it much but I know you care about me, especially when people try to take me down. Feel free to show it more . . .

There are so many other friends I'm grateful for but this part would be chapters long if I don't stop. Please know that this journey would totally suck without you guys. Some of you are working at FV or have worked at FV before, or have helped Fadza and I in many ways, and we will always be grateful. If you ever need us for anything at all, you know you can always call Fadza.

Colleagues in the FV Group, please forgive me if I didn't or couldn't mention your names in this book; your names are in my heart #alsoIdontwanttogetfavoritismaccusations. I hope you read this book and feel so proud that despite all the challenges, we all survived. So many people out there are waiting for us to make mistakes and pounce on us when we do, but it's made us even stronger as a unit. Fadza and I are so indebted to you for all that you do in the company, day in and day out, that we don't even mind those long coffee breaks you guys take. Thank you for sticking by us through all the ups and downs, and I look forward to an equally crazy second decade together. And no, there is no holiday for the launch of this book. Get back to work.

To ex-colleagues of FV, thank you for being a part of our journey and helping us on this crazy ride. You are always missed! Except for the ones who went to competitors. Just kidding. Maybe not kidding.

A special shoutout has to be given to my personal assistant, Ida, my colleague Aliesha and my editor-turned-friend Kak Syida—for without the three of you, this book would never have happened. So thank you for pushing me to start and cheering for me all the way to the finish line!

To my blog readers and to our customers, you have no idea how much you have helped not only us at FV, but also the entire entrepreneurship industry in general. It's because of people like you that dreamers like me get to dream: we get to create jobs, we get to put food on our table and other people's tables, and I thank you for your endless support. You and your credit card details are the entire reason I even have a career, and I will never ever forget that. I hope I can continue to make you proud, and I will try my best to fight with my finance team to make sure we can give you more discounts.

To local brands, local designers and the entire local fashion industry, thank you for all the memories and friendships we have made on this journey. Together, we grew from ground zero, always trying our best to elevate one another. I hope FashionValet helped you on your journey, even if in the smallest way and I'm sorry if we ever disappointed you. I will always be rooting for you, and I hope you'll be rooting for me too.

To everyone who has helped me and FV in this journey, it would be impossible for me to name each one of you. But you know who you are. Partners, investors, suppliers, landlords, mentors, fellow entrepreneurs, Endeavor team and network, media, my social media followers, celebrity friends, social media influencers, other friends and family—I thank you from the bottom of my heart. Please forgive me if I didn't mention your names here, I promise I won't get mad if you write a book and forget to put me in too.

To my publisher, Penguin, it has always been my dream to write a book, so thank you for taking a chance on this girl. Especially to Nora, thank you for putting up with my always-extended deadlines and the constant 'can I just edit that one part . . .'. If this book ever gets made into a movie (and Anne Hathaway plays me), popcorn's on me.

Now on to the most difficult thank you, because it's the biggest one. To my husband, my best friend, my soulmate, my partner in love, work and life, Fadzarudin Anuar—even typing this sentence brought tears to my eyes. It has been a crazy journey of more than ten years of working together and even more amazing *sixteen* years of being together. I can't even begin to tell you how much you mean to me and how grateful I am that you hit on me and said 'I love you' first (if you want to dispute this, write your own book). No one knows more than you, every detail of my first decade, every pain and every joy, because whatever I felt, you felt it too. Together, we charted our path into the unknown and as scary as it was, it's always easier because I have you by my side. Thank you for always encouraging me to chase my dreams, be it at work, at writing my book, at anything at all. You are always my support through it all. Thank you for marrying me and for our beautiful children—I will try to stop at four. Thank you for loving me and always telling me that my cooking is delicious or that I look skinny when I'm nine months pregnant and swollen from water retention. Thank you for all the hard work, sacrifice and effort to make me the happiest woman alive. You are my everything. Can't wait to go through many more decades of life with you, by each other's side, old and grey together.

And last but not least, to YOU. Yes, you reading this. However this book landed in your hands, I am eternally grateful that it's brought you here. I wrote this book to share my entrepreneurship learnings with others, especially those going through their own journeys. It's an extremely lonely path, so I hope I made it a little less lonely for you. We're all in it together, each of us yearning for success, and I truly hope we'll all find it one day. I hope this book also opens doors for more entrepreneurs to tell their stories, and when you do, just freaking hire a ghostwriter. #haha

If you've read this far already, that means you must really like me. So go on and follow me at @vivyyusof on Instagram and our brands @theduckgroup and @lilit_woman. We'll catch up there from hereon!